595

THE NEW COMPLETE
BEAGLE

by HENRY J. COLOMBO
A. D. HOLCOMBE
LEW MADDEN
OWEN PAYNE
MORGAN WING, JR.

1971—Revised Edition

HOWELL BOOK HOUSE INC.

845 THIRD AVENUE, NEW YORK, N.Y. 10022

Ch. Robino II, the top sire of the early 1900s, *from a painting by G. Muss-Arnolt.*

2

Contents

3

1971 Beagle Advisory Committee, American Kennel Club. Back row, l. to r.: Norman J. Furber (Field Trial Department of the AKC), Sidney Check (AKC), Junior S. Sternberg, T. A. Mayberry, Roland Scherer, Thomas J. Keegan, Russell C. Carlson, Willard Deason, John H. Forshar, Arthur E. Curran, William F. Stifel (Executive Secretary of the AKC), John Prianti and Harold Smith. Seated: Robert A. Bartel (AKC Field Representative), John A. Brownell (Vice-President of the AKC), Henri Prunaret, Leonard Luber, A. P. (Bud) Mitchell (AKC Field Representative), and Clifford Knabe.

Acknowledgments

The publisher of this new edition of THE COMPLETE BEAGLE concurs wholeheartedly in the appreciation expressed by William Denlinger in the first edition for the magnificent contributions of the following Beagle authorities:

Mr. Richardson Harwood, National Beagle Club Delegate to the American Kennel Club, for his counsel and review of the manuscript which have been of inestimable value in making THE COMPLETE BEAGLE a highly regarded work.

Mr. Henry J. Colombo for his chapter *Cottontail Field Trials.* Mr. Colombo has served as Secretary of the New England Association of Beagle Clubs, Delegate to the Beagle Advisory Committee, Secretary and President of the Eastern Massachusetts Beagle Club.

Mr. A. D. Holcombe for his chapter *Hare Stakes.* A keen student of hare Hounds and hare trials, Mr. Holcombe has written several books and magazine articles on Beagle families and Beagling.

Mr. Owen M. Payne for his chapter *Training the Beagle for Field Work.* A foremost field trial judge, and breeder-handler of several successive generations of field champions, Mr. Payne served as member of the Beagle Advisory Committee and President of the International Beagle Federation.

Mr. Morgan Wing, Jr., for his chapter *Beagle Packs.* Mr. Wing has served for many years as Secretary of the National Beagle Club, Joint Master of the Sandanona Beagles and Joint Master of the famous Buckram Beagles. In this edition he gives the latest information on Beagle Packs.

Gaines Dog Research Center for the drawings by Paul Brown which appeared in Gaines' *The Beagle.*

For this new edition special thanks are certainly due to:

Mr. Lew Madden for his most informative and useful chapters on *The Gun Beagle, The Field Trial Beagle, The Field Trial Beagler,* and *Judging Field Trials.* Mr. Madden, a field trial judge of note over many years and breeder of many fine field and bench Beagles, is Contributing Editor to *Hounds and Hunting.*

Mr. Ivan W. Carrel and Mr. Robert F. Slike, Editor and General Manager respectively of *Hounds and Hunting,* for their splendid cooperation in providing photographs and engravings for the pictorial section, "Hall of Fame."

ELSWORTH S. HOWELL

5

Clarence Jones, master breeder of the famed Fish Creek Beagles, posing Field Champion Brophy's Miss Webster.

Foreword

Natick, Massachusetts

Pride in their Hounds and eagerness to share in their sport are traditions of Beaglers everywhere. The reader will treasure the lore in THE COMPLETE BEAGLE.

In its pages recognized authorities have compiled all the helpful information which will be invaluable to the novice. Certainly, their interesting discussions of the various phases of Beagling will stimulate provocative thought among all fanciers. Containing a fine collection of pictures, the result is a book that will be referred to over and over again.

THE COMPLETE BEAGLE is a tribute to the devotion of those faithful friends who contribute the knowledge gathered through years of experience. May we all, good Houndsmen old and new, enjoy many happy hours with the Merry Little Beagles.

RICHARDSON HARWOOD
National Beagle Club Delegate
to The American Kennel Club

From a 17th century engraving by F. Barlow.

The History And Development of the Beagle

IN tracing the history of any breed of dogs, many difficulties are encountered. Prior to the time the first dog shows were held and the first studbooks were established in Europe, few authentic records devoted to dogs were kept. While various breeds of dogs were mentioned in publications prior to that time, in most cases the writers were concerned not with the breed itself, but rather with some phase of human life that involved the use of the breed. Then too, a breed might be known by one name in one country while dogs of a very similar type would be known by another name in another country—yet the two would be fundamentally the same, either having evolved from the same forebears, or the one breed having developed from the other.

Onomasticon, a Greek dictionary in ten books, by Iulius Pollux, Greek grammarian and sophist of the second century A.D., is the earliest surviving work that mentions the use of the dog in connection with the hunting of other animals. This tells that the dog was used for hunting purposes about two hundred years after the promulgation of the Levitical Law, which would be about 1300 B.C. However, geologists believe that it was about 5000 B.C. that man first cap-

9

tured a four-legged animal with twice his own speed, tamed it, and trained it for the purpose of adding to his own powers of tracking, trapping, and killing. Some believe that the dog is a member of the jackal or wolf family, but others believe that there has always been a dog. Whatever his origin, the dog became almost a necessity to man of ancient times who maintained his food supply by hunting down and killing wild animals.

As man's methods of obtaining game developed, the type of dog he wanted was changed to complement his own hunting ability. A dog with the ability to cover ground rapidly was not necessary when man hunted on foot using primitive weapons. As nets came into use, and later firearms, man needed dogs of a different type, so he paired dogs that had to some degree the qualities he most desired, in the hope that the offspring would have the same qualities but to an accentuated degree. So it was that dogs were developed and bred to fit into man's changing way of life. As methods of hunting changed, a particular type of dog might be discarded entirely only to deteriorate and become extinct, or it might be crossbred with other types of dogs, retaining many of its original physical characteristics but fitting better the purpose of its master.

Among the remains of prehistoric civilizations, crude records have been found depicting men hunting with dogs. Often, fanciers of a particular breed will attempt to prove that their own dogs show a marked resemblance to those pictured or described in ages past, thus proving that the breed has existed in its present form for many centuries. Certainly it is questionable whether the crude artistry of long ago portrayed the dog exactly as he appeared at the time. In addition, it is questionable whether any breed has remained unchanged in physical characteristics for any great number of years.

Despite the fact that the ancestry of a particular breed cannot be proved positively, the history of any breed, its probable physical development, its use through the years, and its place in the life of man are extremely fascinating subjects.

10

From the time of prehistoric man, when hunting was primarily a means of procuring food to sustain life, civilization gradually advanced to the point where hunting became, instead, a sport. For centuries, hunting was exclusively a pastime of royalty and the landed aristocracy. Considered a personalized hobby, it called for fine clothes, elaborate equipment, and the best of Hounds. The Hounds varied in type from the large breeds used for hunting deer to the small breeds used for hunting hare.

Hare hunting was described as a popular sport in England as early as the fourteenth century. Edward the Third of England (1312-1373) was said to have been such a devotee of hunting that even during the war between England and France he had a pack of sixty couple of hare Hounds with him in the French Dominion. While it may be safely assumed that these hare Hounds were of the Beagle type, and were, without doubt, the progenitors of our present-day Beagle, the breed name was not used in describing these early hare Hounds.

The earliest mention of the Beagle (by that name) in English literature apparently is in the "Esquire of Low Degree," which was published in 1475:

> "With theyr beagles in that place
> And seven score raches at his rechase."

In the fifteenth century there is frequent reference to the Beagle, and in the sixteenth century, the following was written, "Frenchmen still like good begeles following their prey."

Why the name Beagle was applied to this particular breed is uncertain. It has been suggested that the word is derived from the old French *bégueule* (which in turn came from the word *béer,* meaning to gape, open wide, and *guele,* meaning throat). That the term "open throat" may have been used to describe this particular breed is plausible. It has also been suggested that the name may have come from the Old English *begle,* the French *beigh,* and the Celtic *Beag*—all three of which mean small.

In *British Dogs,* Hugh Dalziel, discussing the origin and history of the breed, made the following statement: "The

11

name Beagle seems to be of doubtful etymology. Skinner derives it from the French bugler, *mugire;* and Menage thinks, as the hounds were sent from Britain into Gaul, the name may be of British origin. Skeat says the term is of unknown origin. Ogilvie gives Beagle from the French *beigle,* so named from littleness. . ."

In describing Beagles, Dalziel began with a quotation from Chaucer:

"Of smallë houndës had she, that she fed
On roasted flesh and wastel bred."

In his *History of the Mastiff,* Wynn had declared that the Normans used the word Harrier, or Harier, to refer to Hounds in general. Dalziel asserted, however, that Chaucer's use of the word houndës rather than Harriers, or Hariers, disproved Wynn's theory, and declared that Chaucer's words refer to the Beagle, the smallest of the Hounds. Dalziel felt that the fact that Chaucer so referred to the breed was in itself an argument against Wynn's contention that Harrier, or Harier, was the general name adopted by the Normans for all Hounds.

Dame Juliana Berners, who is accepted as an authority on hunting in her day, and who wrote a century after Chaucer did, included neither Beagle nor Harrier (by those names) in the list of dogs she published, which is as follows: "The names of divers manere of houndes, These ben the names of houndes: Fyrste, there is a Grehounde, a Bastard, a Mongrell, a Mastife, a Lemor, a Spanyell, Raches, Kennettys, Terours, Butcher's houndes, Dunghill dogges, Tyrndel Tayles, and Pruyckered Curres and smalle Ladyes Popees, that bere away the fleas and divers smale fawtis."

Dalziel asserts that Raches are closely identical with the Harrier, and that the term is so used by Edmund de Langley, author of "Mayster of Game," who wrote about the time of Chaucer. Dalziel could find no reference to the Beagle prior to the time of Queen Elizabeth, but stated that Skeat refers the word to "The Squire of Low Degree," which he had not read. He also said that the term "Kennettys," or "Kenet," was given in Wright and Thomas's *Dictionary of Obsolete and Provincial English* as meaning a small Hound, and would, therefore, most appropriately apply to the Beagle.

Because the Kennettys (or Kenets) were described as small dogs of the Hound type, and the name is said to have meant "low, or of low degree," other authorities besides Dalziel have suggested that the Kennettys were actually Beagles. Kennettys are known to have existed in numbers during the time of Edward the Confessor (about the eleventh century), and their general physical structure and character have led to the suggestions that there is a close relationship between them and the Segusian, or Basset, as well as the Dachshund and the Beagle.

In the forest laws of King Canute, certain dogs are prohibited within the royal forests, but exemption is especially made of the Veltever, "which the English call Langehren (long-eared), for, manifestly, they are too small to do any harm"—that is, harm to the king's deer. The Veltever, Dalziel felt, must have been the Beagle.

Bewick's Quadrupeds (1790) describes the Beagle as the smallest of the dogs kept in England for the chase, and declares that the Beagle "is only used in hunting the hare; although far inferior in point of speed to that animal, they follow by the exquisiteness of their scent, and trace her footsteps through all her various windings with such exactness and perseverance, that they afford most excellent diversion, and generally reward the hunter's toil with the death of the wearied fugitive. Their tones are soft and musical, and add greatly to the pleasures of the chase."

In England during the Middle Ages, two varieties of Hounds existed in great numbers. These were known as Northern Hounds and Southern Hounds. In addition to these two, there were also those of a larger type used for trailing deer, and some of a smaller type (which are presumed to have been Harriers and Beagles) used for trailing hare. Stag hunting and hare hunting were popular during this period, and Hounds used for hare were hunted in packs and were followed on foot.

The Beagle is known to have existed in England in numbers during Elizabethan times, and it is said to have been

13

popular during the immediately preceding period when Henry VIII reigned. Not only are there written records of the Beagle during the reign of Queen Elizabeth (1533-1603), but also there are pictures existing today which show members of her Royal Court hunting with Beagles, as well as a portrait of Queen Elizabeth which shows her with a Beagle at her left.

The Beagles depicted in these paintings were said to have been carried in the gauntlets and the saddle panniers of hunters on horseback. They have been variously described as ranging in height from eight to twelve inches at the shoulder.

Hare hunting on horseback was enjoyed by England's King James I (1566-1625). A contemporary described his hunting thus: "live hares in baskets being carried to the Heath, made excellent sport for His Majesty." His regard for the merry little Beagles who accompanied him was obviously high, for King James praised his favorite minister, Cecile, Earl of Salisbury, for his wisdom and his ability to scent out plots by referring to him as "My little Beagle."

Although the writings of this time indicate that the Beagle was a popular breed, they also indicate that the Beagle was somewhat lacking in the life and spirit reflected in other breeds of dogs used for hunting purposes. The Beagle appealed more to those satisfied to hunt in a rather restrained manner, in contrast to hunters who were interested in game of larger types and who required dogs characterized by the ability to perform with greater speed and dash.

No doubt the English Beagles of the past comprised several varieties for even now packs of English Beagles differ somewhat as to size. Those usually followed on foot are smaller and consequently not so fast as the larger varieties. At one time, English Beagles were described as two distinctly different breeds—the rough-coated and the smooth-coated. King George IV (1762-1830) was an ardent admirer of the smooth-coated Beagle and during the period when he was Prince of Wales frequently hunted with this type; his pack of dwarf Beagles was considered an institution on Brighton Downs. What is considered to be one of the best portraits

14

of George IV shows him surrounded by his merry little pack, each member of which shows marked conformity with the typical Beagle of the present day.

The small Beagle of the Elizabethan period evidently did not remain popular for long, although these Hounds were said to have had keen noses and musical voices as well as the ability to hunt well in packs. Apparently, speed was not one of their attributes, but they were said to have possessed great stamina in spite of their small size and to have followed a trail with persistance. Just what strains of the breed existed at that time is not known.

Writers of the seventeenth century mentioned a North Country Beagle which was said to be faster and more slender than the Cotswold Beagle, and about 1700, William Somerville (1675-1742) described the characteristics of the Cotswold Beagle of his day and told how he had bred some of his best Harriers by crossing the Cotswold Beagle with the old Southern Hound.

Somerville, often termed the poet of the chase, advocated "a different Hound for every different chase," and poetically described the tactics of the hare as well as the tactics of the Hounds and the hunters. Among his verses which express the joy of the hunt, are the following lines:
"Pour down, like a flood from the hills, brave boys,
   On the wings of the wind
   The merry beagles fly;
   Dull sorrow lags behind:
   Ye shrill echoes reply,
 Catch each flying sound, and double our joys."

In France during the reign of the Bourbons, the lavishness of the chase was unparalleled. At Chantilly, where Prince Louis Henry de Bourbon maintained his residence, records of the sport have been preserved. The records from 1748 to 1779 show that 77,750 hare were accounted for in the chase, as compared with 3,364 stags and hinds, the next ranking game.

Beckford wrote about 1750 that the Fox-Beagle was exceptionally lively, light and fleet of foot, and told how he crossed his Harriers with this type of Beagle to produce

15

dogs with greater dash and drive. Some time earlier, the Beagle had been compared with the Foxhound by Beckford, who said: "The Beagle will puzzle an hour on one spot sooner than leave the scent; while the Foxhound, full of life and spirit is always dashing and trying forward." While this may have been intended as an unfavorable criticism of the Beagle, the Beagle's tenacity in refusing to leave the scent might well be considered a desirable characteristic by others who were less interested in a dog whose assets were greater speed and increased alacrity. Early descriptions of the breed portray a picture somewhat different from our Beagle of today. If those earlier dogs actually were, as they have been described, long of back, short and bent of leg, with long ears and a short neck, the breed may have deserved some criticism and ridicule.

The *Sportsman's Cabinet* published in 1803 includes a description of the Beagle and the breed's development. This stresses the fact that although the breed has undergone different distinctions in proportion to the size the Beagle has been bred, and despite the fact that it may have been considered judicious to cross the Beagle with other breeds, the Beagle's outstanding ability to scent game has, from time immemorial, been joyfully expressed by each individual dog in what has come to be "exultingly called the exhilarating cry of the jovial pack."

The article indicates that shortly prior to that time, the breed's popularity had declined, and packs of Beagles had most frequently been in the possession of gentlemen whose age or infirmities had prevented their enjoyment of forms of hunting requiring more strenuous activity. The breed's ability to scent the hare and its vigilance and perseverance in pursuit of its prey were described as causing the Beagle to follow the hare "through all her windings, unravel all her mazes, explore her labyrinths, and by the scent alone trace and retrace her footsteps to a degree of admiration that must be seen to be properly understood; during all of which the soft and melodious tone of their emulous vociferation seems to be the most predominant inducement to the well-known ecstatic pleasures of the chase."

16

It was pointed out that this slow form of hunting was admirably adapted to "age and the feminine gender—that it could be enjoyed by ladies of the greatest timidity as well as gentlemen laboring under infirmities." Even though the hunters might fall behind, there was little possibility of their having to drop out of the hunting party entirely. In addition, a Beagle pack was well suited to the hunting expeditions of the neighboring rustics, who, possessing no horses, could readily keep up with the pack on foot.

The breeders of that time were said to have been interested primarily in producing a Beagle as small as possible, yet representing the greatest merit with respect to physical structure. Even among professed amateurs, every effort was made to attain perfection, and in this they were said to have generally been successful. The Beagles of the various packs were so uniformly well matched with respect to height that they did not exceed ten or eleven inches in height; so carefully were they selected with respect to speed, that whenever they were running, they might be covered with a sheet. Although the dogs were slow, and in the beginning were usually some distance behind the hare, so persistant were the members of the pack that the chase inevitably ended with the hare meeting death even though three or four hours might be required before the quarry was finally caught. But as the trend in hunting practices changed and the hunter's desire for speed increased, the popularity of the Beagle waned until at the beginning of the nineteenth century, it was uncommon to see a pack of any great size.

The numerous crosses of different breeds of both Beagles and Hounds are discussed in the *Sportsman's Cabinet* (1802) to some extent, but without naming the specific breeds involved, other than to mention the crossing of Beagles and Foxhounds. These two breeds are said to have been crossed repeatedly to produce the Harrier of that day—a dog of increased size and speed. Other crosses are mentioned as having been made for the purpose of producing Beagles better adapted for the soil and surface over which they were intended to hunt. These were said to have ranged from the one extreme, the old, heavy, deep-tongued, dewlapped

17

Southern Hound of Lancashire (where the huntsman with his long pole followed on foot) to the completely divergent type, the fleetest bred Northern Harriers of the day whose rapidity was but little inferior to coursing.

Although the Harrier is described as the product of the crossing of the Beagle and the Foxhound, it is explained that the Beagle, in the sporting meaning of the term, is not to be considered synonymous with the Harrier. In spite of the fact that the two breeds possessed precisely the same properties, the Beagle was much smaller in size. The pack of Col. Hardy is described as an impressive example of how diminutive was the early Beagle. Each member of this collection of Beagles, which consisted of "ten or twelve couple," was so tiny that the entire group was carried to and from the hunt in a single pair of panniers slung across a horse. Small as they were, and insignificant as they perhaps would now seem, they were still capable of following the hare through all its efforts at escape, finally worrying (or teasing) it to death. This tiny pack was kenneled in a small barn which one night was broken open and every Hound, as well as the panniers, was stolen. Despite the most diligent search, no trace of the thieves or their loot was ever found.

The *Sportsman's Cabinet* published in 1804 explains that in some counties, Beagles both rough and smooth were admired, provided they had been properly selected and were well matched. Their tongues are described as musical and their indefatigable and unremitting bustle as entertaining. Their running so close to the ground is mentioned as one advantage the Beagles had over taller dogs, for this enabled them to imbibe and enjoy the scent sooner, especially when the air was dense. In an enclosed country, Beagles were expected to hunt most creditably, for their patience in trailing, their alertness at a fault, their perseverance in haws and hedge-rows were then employed to the utmost. It is pointed out, however, that a steady, philosophic huntsman was required, for sometimes twenty-five couples might be classed together, with not ten to be depended upon. The sportsman seeking a pre-eminent pack was advised to select dogs of medium size, with a back rather broad than round;

nose wide and flat, with open, well-distended nostrils; chest deep and capacious; fillets firm and prominent; haunches large and muscular; hams straight; feet round, the sole hard and dry; claws large; ears wide, silkily pendulous, thin, and more round than pointed at the extremities; eyes full; forehead broad; upper lips thick, and deeper than the under jaw; and in striving to produce Hounds having unison of tongue, symmetry in size, and uniformity of figure and speed, the breeder was advised that too much care and inspection could not be bestowed upon the choice of sires and dams to be used for propagation.

William Youatt, in his book *The Dog* published in 1846, agreed that the origin of the Beagle is somewhat obscure, but felt that the breed evolved from the Harrier and the old Southern Hound, with a decided decrease of size and speed, yet possessing an exceedingly musical voice and a very great power to scent. Although he explained that close running was considered a mark of excellence in Hounds of every kind, Youatt described the Beagles of his day as rarely more than ten or twelve inches in height and so uniform in size and power of speed that it was commonly said a running pack might be covered with a sheet.

Youatt recalled with pleasure the day when the good old English gentleman used to keep his pack of Beagles or little Harriers, slow but sure, occasionally carried to the field in a pair of panniers on a horse's back. Often an object of ridicule at an early period of the chase, they rarely failed to accomplish their purpose, "the puzzling pack unravelling wile by wile, maze within maze." Despite the fact that two or three hours might be required to accomplish this, it was seldom, Youatt said, that the hare did not fall victim to her pursuers.

Youatt explained that the Beagle was fleeter than its diminutive size would indicate, and also that the breed possessed all the strength and endurance necessary to ensure their killing game. After a period in which, as a result of its comparative lack of speed, the breed's popularity had gradually declined to the point where the Beagle's use as a hunting dog was almost totally discontinued, this diminu-

19

tive Hound had returned to favor, especially in the royal park at Windsor.

Youatt stated further that great care had formerly been exercised in breeding these dogs which were distinguished by the names "deep-flewed" or "shallow-flewed," depending upon whether they were characterized by the larger upper lip of the Southern Hound or the shallow-flewed, more contracted lip of the Northern dogs. The shallow-flewed, Youatt described as the swiftest Beagles; the deep-flewed as the stoutest and surest, and the strain having the most pleasant voices. The wire-haired Beagles were considered by Youatt as the stouter and better dogs.

Youatt said that the form of the head of the Beagle had been much misunderstood, and that it should be large, decidedly round, and thick rather than long, that there then would be room for the expansion of the nasal membranes which are responsible for the ability to scent and for the reverberation of sound. The latter he described as peculiarly pleasant in the Beagle.

Stonehenge, in the fifth edition of the *Manual of British Sports* (1861), declared that the Harrier and Beagle may be considered together, for they were at that time so much bred one with the other that it was difficult to say which were Harriers and which were Beagles. The Beagle he described as the more specific breed, and pointed out that the hare, unlike the fox, is constantly "doubling," that is, returning upon its track in an effort to foil its pursuers. To meet this artifice, Stonehenge said, an exquisite nose was required, together with great patience and considerable cunning. Hence, the hare Hound differed from the Foxhound in that the former possessed an acuter sense of smell, a slower pace, less dash, and more patience; it was also necessary that the hare Hound be able to distinguish a "heel-scent;" otherwise, he might return upon the hunted line, fancying that he was following a "double" of the hare. Stonehenge also stressed the fact that hare Hounds must "pack closely," for as the hare doubles back, a widely spread pack might lose the scent of its prey.

Declaring that the Beagle, embodying all these points of

20

perfection, is the model hare Hound of the old school, Stonehenge described the breed as ranging in height from ten inches (or even less) to fifteen. In shape, he said, they resembled the old Southern Hound in miniature, but with more neatness and beauty, and with a comparable style of hunting. In a more detailed comparison, Stonehenge described the head and ears of the Beagle as much broader than the Foxhound, the ears longer, more nearly comparable to the Bloodhound in development; the legs shorter; the body bigger and stouter; and the breed very hardy and capable of an immense amount of work.

At the two extremes of the Beagle subdivision, Stonehenge said, stand the dwarf Beagle—a little smooth lap dog with very long ears and almost pug nose—and the Fox Beagle, which resembled the Foxhound in all but size and dash. He listed patience, cooperation, freedom from jealousy, goodness of nose, and Lilliputian dimensions as the essential qualities of the breed. The varieties of the breed, Stonehenge summed up as follows: first, the medium Beagle, which may be either heavy and Southern-like, or light and Northern-like; second, the dwarf or lap dog Beagle; third, the Fox Beagle; and fourth, the rough or Terrier Beagle.

In his third edition of *The Dog*, published in 1872, Idstone indicated that general standards for the conformation of the "toys" had been established some seventy years before by the London fancy, but that Stonehenge's book was the first publication which gave fixed rules for breeding to perfection. The dog shows, he said, originated about 1859 or 1860 and enabled breeders to get together to compare notes and learn from competition.

Describing "Lilac" (a bitch), Idstone said she was as good a model as could be found, "somewhere about ten inches, with a Hound-tan head, deep thick flexible ears drooping almost to her shoulders, well hung, flat to her head, and a rich black-and-white body and fine stern, slightly hooped—in short, with more prominent ears than the Foxhound, but in other respects a *bijou* model of that grandest of the canine race."

Idstone mentioned no other individual Beagle as especially outstanding, although he described several Beagle packs of which he had personal knowledge. The packs were described as of no particular height, but as reminding one of the old saying, "high, low, Jack, and the game." One pack, which belonged to a very large, lame wine merchant, was described as consisting of ten couples, varying from about 13½ inches to 11 inches in height, and as having been used for hunting bagged rabbits turned out on a meadow.

At the time the book was written, said Idstone, probably the best pack ever seen or bred was kept by Mr. James Crane of Southover House, near Dorchester. At Idstone's request, Mr. Crane exhibited these Beagles once or twice with complete success. Mr. Crane's standard was a height of nine inches, and as a result of the wonderful hindquarters and general frame and development, the dogs were able to account for a rabbit in approximately five minutes. The variety of color in this pack of Beagles (which were perfectly level "at trough" and in their speed) added to their beauty, in Idstone's opinion. To him, it also proved that they were identical in family lines with the Southern Hound or Harrier. One or two, he said, were of a genuine Harrier appearance, especially a blue mottle, quite free from all black patches, with a Hound-tan head. Many were mottled with larger markings. Yellows and hare-pieds were encouraged and much fancied by Mr. Crane, for in attaining a kennel standard of nine inches, he looked for qualities he considered more important than color. In establishing the pack, points of conformation which interested Mr. Crane most were: size; symmetry; straightness of limbs; length of ear; quality of voice and nose; sagacity; substance; and muscular quarters.

Dogs: Their Points, Whims, Instincts, and Peculiarities, edited by Henry Webb, compares the number of Beagles in proportion to the total dogs entered at two important nineteenth century English dog shows—the show at the Holborn Horse Repository, held on October 1, 2, 3, and 4, 1861, and the show held at the Crystal Palace in 1871, just ten years later. In each of these shows, nine Beagles were entered. In the 1861 show, there was a total of 240 dogs entered in

22

forty-eight classes, whereas in the 1871 show, there was a total of 834 dogs entered in one hundred and ten classes. Whether this may be interpreted as a general decrease in the breed's popularity is a matter of conjecture, for the book includes no conclusive statement to that effect.

In 1872, Idstone wrote that contemporary Beagle breeding programs were concerned with purity both as to type and as to breed characteristics. At that period, the breeding of Beagles on English estates was confined to the dogs each owned, with little intermingling of strains. Thus were developed the individual strains which even today remain extant.

In 1892 a joint studbook of packs of Beagles and Harriers was published in England. The first volume contained the names of only a dozen Beagle packs. Although this supposedly represented all of the foundation stock, it is probable that at least double that number of packs were then in existence in England.

The American Book of the Dog, edited by G. O. Shields and published in 1891, describes the increased popularity of the Beagle as an American field dog and attributes this to the fact that game birds had at that time been so nearly exterminated that sportsmen were discarding their bird dogs. In their place, the hunters were using the Beagle, a breed whose natural game (the rabbit and the hare) was so plentiful that even in the vicinity of large cities a satisfying and successful hunt could be enjoyed.

It is not to such circumstances alone, however, that the Beagle's continued popularity should be attributed. Stamina, persistence, and exceptional ability to scent are breed characteristics as highly esteemed today as they were in the days of Good Queen Bess. And the merry music of the Beagle's tongue, unchanged through the passing years, remains a hypnotic signal inspiring his enthusiastic followers to join him in the chase that is about to begin.

Harry T. Peters, owner of the famous Windholme Beagles of the early 1900s (see pages 30 and 31). This painting of Mr. Peters, done in 1932 during his Mastership of the Meadowbrook Hounds, is by F. B. Voss.

Louis Batjer, whose Meadow Lark Beagles were particularly important on the American show scene in the 1930s. Among them were Ch. Meadow Lark Watchman and Ch. Meadow Lark Fear Not, Best Sporting at Westminster in 1930 and 1931, the last two years that Beagles were shown in the Sporting Group.

Early American Bloodlines

AMONG the early American records dating back to Colonial times when groups of Europeans searching for religious freedom were emigrating to this land of hope and promise, we find mention of the fact that dogs of various breeds were often brought along to help the settlers in their efforts to conquer the wild new land and provide for themselves a more favorable life. Some of the dogs served as guards, some assisted their masters by drawing heavily laden carts, and others helped the settlers in their hazardous struggle to secure game for food. For the latter purpose the settlers brought dogs whose outstanding attributes were the ability to scent, to trail, and to capture game.

Obviously, our early American settlers were more interested in the practical ability of the dogs than in the quality of their breeding. Doubtless many of these dogs were of mixed breeding, although some were of breeds that are now classed in the Hound Group, for we find occasional mention of dogs by specific breed names. For obvious reasons, the owners of these dogs were not particularly concerned with promoting a program of selective breeding, and undoubtedly a great many of the offspring from these first imported dogs were the result of accidental, or at best, careless, matings. With each succeeding generation, the breed characteristics became less obvious and the bloodlines more mixed. As time went on, these poorer specimens, representing a conglomeration of breeds, came to be looked upon as natives of this continent, although such was not actually the case.

In most instances, the mention of dogs in early American records was incidental to the subject of the records, so it was only rarely that the dogs were mentioned by breed names. Probably the first mention of the Beagle by that name is to be found in the historical records of the city of Ipswich, Massachusetts. Originally known as Aggawam, this settlement came into being in 1633. Incorporated in 1634 as Ipswich, the town was probably among the better organized of the period, and many of its records have been preserved to the present day as part of the collection of the historical society kept in the John Whipple House, the oldest of the seventeenth century houses still existing in Ipswich. Joseph Barlow Felt's *History of Ipswich, Essex, and Hamilton,* published in 1834, was based in part upon these early town records. Included in the book is the following excerpt from the records for the year 1642:

"Whosoever kills a wolf is to have . . . the skin, if he nail the head up at the meeting-house and give notice to the constables. Also, for the better destroying or fraying away the wolves from the town, it is ordered that by the 1st day of the 7th month, every house holder whose estate is rated 500 pounds and upward, shall keep a sufficient mastive dog; or 100 pounds to 500 pounds, shall provide a sufficient hound or beagle to the intent that they be in readiness to hunt and be employed for the ends aforesaid."

As our country progressed and the struggle to exist became less arduous, the more prosperous of our people began to have time to enjoy life. It was only to be expected that their sporting pursuits should follow, in so far as was possible, the patterns then in vogue among the wealthier Europeans of the day. Following Hounds on horseback in the pursuit of wild game became a popular pastime, grad-

26

ually assuming an almost serious aspect in the lives of the landed aristocracy. In the beginning, these hunters were forced to use whatever dogs were available locally. But as time passed, the hunt itself became a secondary concern and the hunters made a concerted effort to acquire better Hounds and more elaborate hunting equipment.

Prior to the Civil War, the hunters in the Southern States used small hunting Hounds to pursue the fox and the hare. Among the Hounds were some that were referred to as Beagles, although they bore but little resemblance to our Beagles of today. Mostly white with a few dark markings, they were described as being more of the Dachshund or Basset type as far as physical conformation was concerned, in spite of the fact that they may actually have borne little resemblance to either of these two breeds. They were said to have had straight legs and comparatively weak heads.

While hunting as a sport was all but forgotten during the war between the States, following the reconstruction period, a resurgence of interest in the use of Hounds in the field took place. Realizing that their own stock was somewhat lacking in fine breed attributes, those hunters who were financially able to do so, imported dogs of the best European strains and made an effort to develop a regulated breeding program. Although owners of good dogs made every effort to avoid careless matings and accidental crossings of breeds, pedigree records for the period are sorely lacking.

Then early in the 1870's, General Richard Rowett, Carlinville, Illinois, became seriously interested in Beagling. From the Beagles he imported stem much of the best of today's network of American Beagle bloodlines. Although we have no records available to prove which English strains his Hounds represented, they may well be assumed to have been from some of the best strains of the time, for contemporary accounts of the Beagles of Rowett's strain vividly portray Hounds of exceptional conformation and intrinsic merit—particularly as compared with the Beagles previously produced by American breeders.

In conjunction with Mr. Norman Elmore, General Rowett

27

embarked upon a serious program of Beagling and Beagle breeding. Even today, the pedigree-conscious Beagler feels it is a feather in his cap to find the name of a Beagle of the Rowett strain in the pedigree of his Hound, no matter how many generations back it may appear.

The Rowett Beagles were noted for their uniformity of type, their excellent bench-show conformation, their evenness of markings, and their ability in the field. Among the early Beagles which were reputedly among Rowett's imported stock, were Rosey, Sam, Dolly, and Warrior. There is some question as to the authenticity of the records which show Rowett as the importer of the latter dog. Some sources point to Warrior as an importation of a Mr. Turner. Regardless of whether Rowett imported this dog, it is generally conceded that his strain was developed from the four dogs named above, and that Dodge's Rattler, or old Rattler, a Hound of great influence in the Rowett strain, was the offspring of Warrior and Rowett's Rosey.

Ringwood and Countess were imported by Mr. Elmore to serve as pillars in the development of the Elmore strain. Ringwood caused a good deal of controversy when some Beaglers raised a question as to the excellence of his type. Despite this adverse criticism, however, the offspring resulting when Ringwood was extensively bred with the Rowett strain included many excellent Beagles, among whom was Comeroe, a dog much lauded for the excellence of his physical conformation, and apparently well deserving the praise he received. Because the extensive inter-breeding of the Rowett and Elmore strains produced such excellent offspring, for a number of years, Beagles of these two strains were considered to be the finest—almost to the exclusion of all others.

For some time after the death of General Rowett, the Rowett Beagles were owned by Mr. Pottinger Dorsey, Newmarket, Maryland, and Mr. C. Staley Doub, Frederick, Maryland. While these two men valued the strain for its ability to produce Hounds of exceptional field merit, they apparently were little interested in entering their dogs in bench shows. And since they sold but few of the dogs, the strain

28

at that time was given less public mention than previously, although its excellence had never waned. Continuing their breeding under the Rowett name, Mr. Dorsey and Mr. Doub numbered among their outstanding dogs, Rally, Rambler, Rosey, Lee, and Venus, to name but a few.

Bowman and Ch. Fitz-Hugh Lee were others of the Rowett strain that exerted a great deal of influence on New England Beagle breeding. Both were extensively used at stud and sired a good many outstanding dogs of the period. Their reputation for excellence was based primarily upon their ability to pass on the mental traits required for field work, their exceptional chests, and excellent bone.

Rattler III, or O'Shea's Champion Rattler, owned by Mr. Dan O'Shea, London, Ontario, Canada, is attributed to Rowett breeding. Among the early Hounds that were of exceptional bench-show merit, Rattler is credited with twenty-three first prizes and cups. It was said that Mr. O'Shea's methods of showing the dog were so advanced for those days, that he could win with Rattler under almost impossible conditions. The statement may have had some basis in fact, for the average handler of the period lacked the finesse that is common today.

About 1880, Mr. Arnold, Providence, Rhode Island, imported a pack of the Royal Rock strain from Northern England. These dogs and their offspring also proved a significant influence on the development of the Beagle in America. Following Mr. James L. Kernochan's importation of a pack of Beagles from England (about 1896), an increasing number of imported Hounds entered the bloodlines picture, and the Beagle's popularity increased at a phenomenal rate.

Mr. A. C. Krueger, Wrightsville, Pennsylvania, imported Champion Bannerman from the kennel of J. Crane, Dorsetshire, England, about 1884. Presumably, the dog was imported expressly to serve the purpose of counteracting the tendency toward excessive size that was then plaguing the Beagle breeders. The strain from which Bannerman descended was said to have been of an average height of nine inches, lightly built, and with cobby bodies. Bannerman's get were criticized by some for the excessive amount of

Supper time for Windholme Kennels puppies.
The most interesting part of the kennels are the puppies.

The Windholme Kennels of Beagles.

The second in a series on America's best kennels, of which the Untermyer Greystone Collie Kennels, in the October issue, was the first.

Ch. Windholme's Faultless, a splendid headed bitch.

THE Windholme Kennels are at Islip on the South Shore of Long Island about fifty miles from New York City. The kennels have about two hundred dogs in them, mostly beagles. There are a few Old English sheepdogs, half a dozen Dalmatians, some excellent Foxhounds, the balance being made up of beagles. Mr. Harry T. Peters, the genial owner, is well known about New York as a judge of horses and dogs at all the leading shows. He is the best-known authority on saddle horses and sporting dogs among the younger set. As an exhibitor of dogs, chickens and horses he has made the name of Windholme famous. Between shows he is well known in New York social life, being a member of the best clubs, among others the Union and the Racquet and Tennis clubs.

His kennels, as previously stated, are located at Islip, L. I., right on the Great South Bay. Windholme, the old Indian name of the place, means "Sandy shores washed by silent waters." And so it is, a beautiful point projecting into the South Bay—bounded on either side by beautiful little inlets, known in that part of the country by the prosaic name of "creek." The fourth side of this ideal park is hemmed in by a high stone and wire fence, so that protected by water on three sides and wire on the fourth the dogs have an ideal place to roam and hunt, without worry to the owner of theft or poison.

To get to the place you pass through a high stone gate with a pretty little English lodge at the side; after passing through the gate one is in England, at least it seems so; there are long vistas of well-kept lawns and typical English hedges on all sides; first, are the stables, where are many notable saddle horses resting on their laurels now that the owner has gone in more extensively for the kennels. Notable among the horses are Champion Lady Leona, twice champion at the National Horse Show, Madison Square Garden, who now has a foal that looks as though it would repeat its mother's triumphs. The race pony stallion, The Orphan, is also there with several of his colts from polo

pony mares, and it looks as though the ideal polo pony stallion had been found.

Then come the cows, a beautiful herd of Jerseys. Then the garden, a great big one copied after one of the most famous gardens of England. Past a long line of hothouses and at last we come to the kennels.

First, the office, an ideal little bungalow filled with cases of ribbons, cups and photographs of the notables who have gone before, stuffed heads, emblematic of famous runs, and gold medal certificates from the Pan-American and St. Louis World's Fairs, where the Windholme Kennels made two clean sweeps. In fact, a little paradise for the dog fancier. From the porch of the office, looking straight out across the South Bay, you see the famous Fire Island Lighthouse, first sight to all travelers of America. To the right is the main kennel with ten separate compartments with a large run for each, all opening into the main exercising yard, which is ten acres, shaded by wild cherry trees and the largest ever seen. Further on come another range of buildings. First, the cook house, where all the food is prepared; then the hospital, and beyond the puppy yards with small shade trees and small individual houses. And back of all these is a tract

Ch. Windholme Robino II, the Champion sire.

of about eighty acres of well-kept woodland, where the rabbit is protected and the young hounds are taught to hunt.

Presiding over this domain are two of the best dog men in the country; first, Clayton Grover, who has been with Mr. Peters for twenty years looking out for the beagles, and who has bred in that time at Windholme more champions than any other man. He is well known to all visitors at the large shows, especially Madison Square Garden, where, dressed in his green hunting livery, he has won the cup for the best pack of beagles with the Windholme Pack ever since there has been a cup offered. The other man in charge is William Saxby, known as the "Dean of the Beagle Fancy." He bred and raised beagles in England and America before most of the present-day beagle owners were born. For many years he showed

Windholme's Bartender.
The best little Beagle in America.

73

30

and ran in the field trials under the name of the Standard Beagle Kennels. About a year ago as there was too much for one man to do at Windholme both Saxby and his kennel were annexed. It is no wonder with three such beagle fanciers as Mr. Peters, Grover and Saxby that a kennel should have success.

The beagles at Windholme are kept on strictly the English principle. "The Pack," the whole kennel, that is, of working hounds, not including brood bitches and pups, is handled as a unit. For years Mr. Peters has been working to obtain the results he has to-day. Unity in color, type, conformation, speed and size. It is no easy matter to get fifty hounds alike in all these respects and takes years of careful breeding and inbreeding.

The beagle as used in America is distinctly the individual. The hunter who shoots his rabbit in front of one, two or three beagles, goes out to kill for food; in England the pack is used; the hare which they hunt there is no more shot at than a fox would be. They are hunted to the death by the pack or they make good their escape. Beagles in England are used as a form of recreation and exercise by the entire community in which they are kept; people

The large puppy yard.
Here are seen the shade tents for the dogs.

wood-Lonely strain with the Lynbroughton strain, or better known as Mr. Johnstone's line of breeding. Both of these lines were originally English and have proved an exceptionally good cross.

Mr. William G. Rockefeller, who owns the Rock Ridge beagles, the kennel second in importance to the Windholme beagles in this country, has used the same cross with great success also, but has not produced as many good ones as Mr. Peters, due largely to the fact that the latter has the best Ringwood-Lonely stud dog; in fact the best stud hound we have ever had in America, namely, Windholme Robino II.

Robino II, himself a champion, is the winner of no end of prizes, and won the gold medal at both the Pan-American and St. Louis Fairs as champion of champions. He is now fourteen years of age, but still sturdy and able to hunt, and nearly every hound in the Windholme Kennels claims him as either a sire, grand sire or great grand sire. There are at present seven champions in the kennels sired by him. We publish a picture of this grand old beagle with this article. The two most famous show and stud beagles of the present day are Champion Windholme's Robino III

Ready for the hunt.
Each dog is all action for the chase.

follow them on foot for sport and exercise. Here in America we climb up on a pile of rocks and wait for our beagle or perhaps a pair of beagles to drive the rabbit around till we get a shot at it.

As before stated, the American beagle is kept for his individuality, his speed, sagacity, etc., as developed by our field trials, which in the general run are only a trial of individual merit. The Windholme beagles are hunted as a pack entirely; game is seldom, if ever, shot before them, and they are used for the sport and recreation of any who choose to follow them.

The pack is exercised regularly, either on foot or on polo ponies, and hunted regularly through the open season, either afoot or from ponies, according to whether the country is easy or difficult to follow it.

The great success of these kennels has been obtained by breeding on the same lines. They have crossed what is known as the Ring-

The undefeated Windholme Pack.
The men in charge of the kennels, Saxby and Grover, are famous beagle authorities.

and Champion Windholme's Matchless, both undefeated, except by kennel mates. Both are sired by Robino II, and through these two the blood lines are being carried out.

Among the younger hounds in the pack are two famous young dogs, Champions Snapshot and Bang, both sired by Matchless, who have made sensations during the last season. Among the bitches are such champions as Faultless, Fearless and many more. The most interesting part of the kennels are the puppies. Each mother has her own little house and yard shaded with dwarf apple and quince trees, where the embryo champions play and exercise to their heart's content. At the time of our visit there were fourteen families in all, with fifty-seven champions in the making to carry on the laurels of the well-known Windholme type. Mr. Peters may well be praised for his efforts to give to America the distinction of having a type which equals anything that has been imported, and from the interest that is being aroused in this miniature foxhound, the future of the beagle is reasonably assured.

Returning home
Tired after their chase through field and wood.

white in their coats, for they were somewhat lacking in the usual Hound markings of black and tan.

Today, Bannerman himself receives but cursory mention by many historians of the breed, although during his own day, his influence on the breed was considered of great significance. He was considered at that time to be the chief rival at stud of Frank Forrest, another Beagle that enjoyed an amazing reputation for the ability to produce outstanding offspring.

Owned by H. L. Kreuder, Champion Frank Forrest consistently produced get with extraordinary field ability. Whether he should be given all the credit for this quality in his offspring is a matter that is open to question, for as his popularity as a stud increased, more and more of the best bitches in the country were mated with him. Obviously, the excellence of the bitches must have played a contributing part in the excellent quality of the resulting litters.

The development of the Blue Cap strain was begun shortly before 1900. This particular strain is still enthusiastically hailed for its ability to produce outstanding field Hounds. The Blue Cap strain owes its development to Mr. Hiram Card, Elora, Canada. One of his foundation studs was Card's Blue Cap, the son of Blue Cap and Blue Bell (or Belle), both imported by Mr. William Asheton, a Virginia Beagling enthusiast, from the English kennels of Sir Arthur Ashburnham. Entirely different in markings from other outstanding Beagle strains, their coats have a good deal of black on the back, the heads show a rich tan color, and the under parts of the body and the legs, a mottled blue and tan ticking. This body coloration led to a discussion as to the purity of their breeding—whether they may have carried the blood of small Foxhounds or the old English Harrier. Impossible though it is today to determine the truth regarding their bloodlines, the Blue Caps' exceptional conformation and excellent field qualities must be given the credit they deserve.

It would be an almost never-ending task to discuss all of the early breeders and the Hounds that have contributed to the excellence of our current strains. Among the early im-

Ch. Windholme's Gamester

Ch. Windholme's Faultless

Ch. Bangle, owned by Harry T. Peters, and described by him as the best Beagle he ever saw. Her win of Best Dog in Show at a Ladies Kennel Association show held in Madison Square Garden near the turn of the century, judged by famous English authority George Raper, may well have been the first Best in Show in America.

33

Ch. Meadow Lark Draftsman, owned by Mrs. William duPont, Jr., winner of the special award given by the American Kennel Club in 1939 for Best American-Bred of All Breeds. Draftsman scored 7 Bests in Show, 42 Hound Group firsts, and 56 Bests of Breed in that year. He was handled by J. Nate Levine.

An early Obedience star was Muscoot Deborah, CD, CDX, UD. "Debby", at left, scored a perfect 200 in finishing her Utility degree in 1939. With her is Ch. Charmac Merrylad. Both were owned by Mrs. Charlotte P. Thornton.

34

ported dogs of particular merit, however, were Chimer, imported by Harry Peters, Islip, New York; Driver (from the kennels of Capt. J. Otho Paget), imported by Eugene Reynel, New York; and the Pullbro Beagles, a wire-haired strain imported about 1883. Bred by Mr. J. W. Appleton, Ipswich, Massachusetts, this strain produced wire-haired and smooth-coated Hounds.

Among other early Beaglers whose breeding programs have had considerable influence on today's outstanding Hounds are H. C. Phipps; George Post; W. E. Deane; C. S. Wixom; F. B. Zimmer; Daniel F. Summers; Edward Marshall; James McAleer; and Chetwood Smith, one of whose Beagles won A.K.C. Field Trial Champion Certificate No. 1.

Today, many Beagles of the past are all but lost in obscurity, despite the fact that they were considered exceptional in their own time. This may be due, at least in part, to the fact that ideas as to desirable conformation have changed somewhat as time passed. Another contributing factor may be that once the original owner died and the strains were dispersed to other kennels, the name of the original strain was superseded by the kennel name of the new owner. Thus the acclaim for excellence of type is given to the strain under its more recent name. To the student of genetics, the influence of these great Hounds of the past is still apparent in the succeeding generations of offspring. But too often, as succeeding generations relegate them to a place further back in the pedigree, our early Beagles are not given the credit they justly deserve.

From the time of the formation of the first Beagle club, and the advent of field trials in the '90's, Beagling assumed a position of paramount importance in the lives of a great many Americans. Today, the Beagle ranks among the most popular breeds in America. The Beagle may be hunted singly, in braces, or in packs. However he is hunted, or if he serves only as a companion to his master, the Beagle's popularity is well deserved.

Sandanona Beagles, Mr. and Mrs. Morgan Wing, Jr., Joint Masters.

From a water color by Michael Lyne, who is a Beagler himself and was master of his own pack in England for some years, this picture shows the Sandanona Beagles in full cry on a hare.

Early English Standards

THE description of the Beagle and the Standard of Points included in *Dogs: Their Points, Whims, Instincts, and Peculiarities,* edited by Henry Webb, and published in England during the latter half of the nineteenth century, provide interesting sidelights on the Beagle's development up to that time:

"The Beagle varies so greatly in size that he must be described as two different types.

"The larger sort is full of symmetry, but he is apt to be 'throaty;' and in other respects he resembles the old southern hound reduced in size. Like him, he has an extraordinary power of scenting; even a cold scent appears evident to him.

"As with the harriers so with the Beagles, the bitches being the most symmetrical; and there are some specimens very closely approaching the comeliness of a Broughey or Corbet harrier.

"The smaller Beagle, known as the rabbit Beagle, is the most elegant of the whole family; and occasionally a diminutive pet example has been exhibited at our dog shows. In some packs the standard has been thirteen and a half inches.

"Captain Hall, of Osmington Lodge, near Weymouth, is

said to hunt a pack of twelve inches, or over. Mr. Henry Pickard Cambridge, of Bloxworth, kept a pack for driving his heath and furze country, about thirteen inches high; and he had amongst his hounds two or more couples of rough Beagles, closely resembling the Otter Hound in miniature. One of these, a bitch called Mischief, a black-tan-and-white hound, came from the kennel of a Mr. Hetty, near Cranbourne. These rough Beagles have the full ear and a thorough hound character about them, but they have not the tongue. Their cry is sharp and ringing, and they have not enough of it. Good judges believe them to have been produced, or to have been bred, by crossing with rough Terriers of some description, and that there is not, and never has been, a rough true Beagle. Yet for work they answered. They will face furze or brambles without flinching, and they are remarkably free from running hares.

"The smaller Beagle is hardly ever used for or with the gun. It is kept entirely to rabbit-hunting; and a pack of six couples, not more than nine inches in height, will run down a rabbit in a few minutes. Hounds of this size must be very powerfully made to get through the thick furze-brakes, and to keep up their work from 11 to 4 o'clock. They must be little working models of the Foxhound, and they should be very powerful in their hindquarters. Indeed, the thighs and muscles in the best hounds appear out of proportion.

"The Beagle's foot is not required to be so round and cat-like as that of the Foxhound and harrier, on account of his reduced weight and the lower speed on which he works. His cry is the most musical of all the hounds."

POINTS

Head   15
Neck   5
Legs   10
Feet   10
Shoulders   20
Back and loin   20
Hindquarters   10
Stern and coat 5
Symmetry and colour   5

In *British Dogs,* Dalziel included the following description and points of Beagles which are by H. A. Clark, Esq., Master of the Cockermouth Beagles:

"*Head,* like that of a Foxhound, not quite so broad across forehead, with sweet, intelligent countenance; the head long, and the nose should not come to a sharp point.

"*Ears* long, and set on low down, and carried close to head; not too broad, and the thinner in the leather the better.

"*Neck* and throat long and lean; but some of the heavier hounds are very loose in throat, and have a deep voice.

"*Shoulders,* long and strong, well clothed with muscle.

"*Chest,* deep and wide; ribs also deep.

"*Back,* strong and wide, and especially wide across loins. Bitches are generally better across loins than dogs, for their size.

"*Hindquarters,* the stronger the better, wide and deep; stern strong at set-on, and tapering, carried high, but not curled.

"*Legs* straight, although for work they are no worse standing a little over on the forelegs; strong of bone; feet round, like those of a cat.

"*Colour,* black, white, and tan; black and white. I had a heavy dog the latter colour, that was always first to find game, and always led. He was well known among the Cumbrians, and they knew his voice, and said: 'Dar, that's auld Duster; we'll have a run noo.' Occasionally, Beagles are the colour of Bloodhounds.

"The Beagle should be hard in condition, with plenty of muscle."

1. Excess of dome—ears set high
2. Correct head
3. Flat skull—muzzle snipey

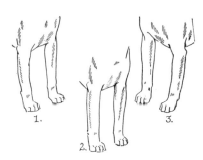

1. Crooked forelegs—down in pasterns
2. Correct forelegs
3. Out at elbows

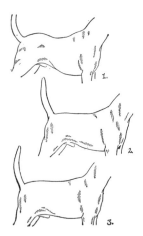

1. Sway back—curved tail
2. Correct back—and body
3. Long back—lacks tuck-up

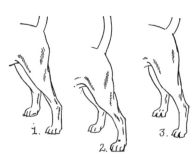

1. Lack of muscle
2. Correct hindquarters
3. Straight hocks—open feet

The AKC Standard of the Breed

(Approved by The American Kennel Club on
September 10, 1957)

Head—The skull should be fairly long, slightly domed at occiput, with cranium broad and full.

Ears—Ears set on moderately low, long, reaching when drawn out nearly, if not quite, to the end of the nose; fine in texture, fairly broad—with almost entire absence of erectile power—setting close to the head, with the forward edge slightly inturning to the cheek—rounded at tip.

Eyes—Eyes large, set well apart—soft and Hound-like—expression gentle and pleading; of a brown or hazel color.

Muzzle—Muzzle of medium length—straight and square-cut—the stop moderately defined.

Jaws—Level. Lips free from flews; nostrils large and open.

Defects—A very flat skull, narrow across the top; excess of dome, eyes small, sharp and Terrier-like, or prominent and protruding; muzzle long, snipey or cut away decidedly below the eyes, or very short. Roman-nosed, or upturned, giving a dish-face expression. Ears short, set on high or with a tendency to rise above the point of origin.

41

BODY—*Neck and Throat*—Neck rising free and light from the shoulders strong in substance yet not loaded, of medium length. The throat clean and free from folds of skin; a slight wrinkle below the angle of the jaw, however, may be allowable.

Defects—A thick, short, cloddy neck carried on a line with the top of the shoulders. Throat showing dewlap and folds of skin to a degree termed "throatiness."

Shoulders and Chest—Shoulders sloping—clean, muscular, not heavy or loaded—conveying the idea of freedom of action with activity and strength. Chest deep and broad, but not broad enough to interfere with the free play of the shoulders.

Defects—Straight, upright shoulders. Chest disproportionately wide or with lack of depth.

Back, Loin and Ribs—Back short, muscular and strong. Loin broad and slightly arched, and the ribs well sprung, giving abundance of lung room.

Defects—Very long or swayed or roached back. Flat, narrow loin. Flat ribs.

FORELEGS AND FEET—*Forelegs*—Straight, with plenty of bone in proportion to size of the Hound. Pasterns short and straight.

Feet—Close, round and firm. Pad full and hard.

Defects—Out at elbows. Knees knuckled over forward, or bent backward. Forelegs crooked or Dachshund-like. Feet long, open or spreading.

Hips, Thighs, Hind Legs and Feet—Hips and thighs strong and well muscled, giving abundance of propelling power. Stifles strong and well let down. Hocks firm, symmetrical and moderately bent. Feet close and firm.

Defects—Cowhocks, or straight hocks. Lack of muscle and propelling power. Open feet.

Tail—Set moderately high; carried gaily, but not turned forward over the back; with slight curve; short as compared with size of the Hound; with brush.

Defects—A long tail. Teapot curve or inclined forward from the root. Rat tail with absence of brush.

Coat—A close, hard, Hound coat of medium length.
Defects—A short. thin coat, or of a soft quality.

Color—Any true Hound color.
General Appearance—A miniature Foxhound, solid and big for his inches, with the wear-and-tear look of the Hound that can last in the chase and follow his quarry to the death.

Scale of Points

Skull	5	
Ears	10	
Eyes	5	
Muzzle	5	
Head	—	25
Neck	5	
Chest and shoulders	15	
Back, loin and ribs	15	
Body	—	35
Forelegs	10	
Hips, thighs and hind legs	10	
Feet	10	
Running Gear	—	30
Coat	5	
Stern	5	
	—	10
Total		100

Varieties—There shall be two varieties. Thirteen Inch—which shall be for Hounds not exceeding 13 inches in height. Fifteen Inch—which shall be for Hounds over 13 but not exceeding 15 inches in height.

Disqualification—Any Hound measuring more than 15 inches shall be disqualified.

PACKS OF BEAGLES
SCORE OF POINTS FOR JUDGING

Hounds—General levelness of pack 40%

Individual merit of Hounds ... 30%

	70%
Manners	20%
Appointments	10%
Total	100%

Levelness of Pack—The first thing in a pack to be considered is that they present a unified appearance. The Hounds must be as near of the same height, weight, conformation and color as possible.

Individual Merit of the Hounds—Is the individual bench-show quality of the Hounds. A very level and sporty pack can be gotten together and not a single Hound be a good Beagle. This is to be avoided.

Manners—The Hounds must all work gaily and cheerfully, with flags up—obeying all commands cheerfully. They should be broken to heel up, kennel up, follow promptly and stand. Cringing, sulking, lying down to be avoided. Also, a pack must not work as though in terror of master and whips. In Beagle packs it is recommended that the whip be used as little as possible.

Appointments—Master and whips should be dressed alike, the master or huntsman to carry horn—the whips and master to carry light thong whips. One whip should carry extra couplings on shoulder strap.

RECOMMENDATIONS FOR SHOW LIVERY

Black velvet cap, white stock, green coat, white breeches or knickerbockers, green or black stockings, white spats, black or dark brown shoes. Vest and gloves optional.

Ladies should turn out exactly the same except for a white skirt instead of white breeches.

What to Look For
and What to Avoid

<table>
<tr><th>Look For:</th><th>Avoid:</th></tr>
</table>

General Type: A dog of the approximate station and proportions as an English (not an American) Foxhound; tremendous, hard bone and intense substance; well knit and with vigor and energy that will enable the Hound to put forth a vast amount of exertion and endure buffets and hardships without injury.

General Type: A weedy, high-stationed dog or one with unduly short legs; weak, fragile bone, shelliness; loosely knit, weak, or lacking animation; any feature that shows signs of weakness or that will impair the Hound's endurance.

Size: Not to exceed 15 inches in vertical measurement from withers to floor at maturity. (Up to 16 inches for such measurement acceptable in England.) Maturity is calculated as one year. Smaller dogs are equally desirable so long as type, substance, bone and vigor are not sacrificed. Breed is divided into two varieties for purposes of exhibition; namely, "over 13 inches and not exceeding 15 inches;" and "not exceeding 13 inches."

Size: Any Hound exceeding 15 inches (16 inches in England) vertical measurement at the withers at maturity.

Color and Markings: Any Hound colors. Usually preferred: white with black and tan (or tan alone) markings; brindle or grizzle superimposed on white acceptable. In the matter of markings, especially upon the head, lateral symmetry is usually deemed desirable, but not essential. Colored eye rims are helpful to the correct expression.

Color and Markings: Absence of any white (not cause for disqualification); any excess of markings that produces a somber aspect. White or flesh-colored eye rims.

45

Look For:	Avoid:
Top Skull or Cranium: Moderately heavy with moderate occipital protuberance. Rounded skull but short of being domed. Refined and exhibiting much quality. Somewhat long, but not excessively so.	**Top Skull or Cranium:** Coarse or exceedingly heavy skull, with absence of occipital protuberance or one of exceeding prominence. Flat skull or excessively domed skull. Absence of refinement or quality in skull. Top skull either very long and narrow or too short and wide.
Foreface or Muzzle: Strong and moderately, but not excessively, carried out. Sharply truncated and square. Neatly chiseled but showing no snipiness. Straight and parallel to top skull.	**Foreface or Muzzle:** Too short or great length. Falling away of under jaw. Tight lips. Filled up under the eyes and without chiseling. Pointed or snipey. Down face or dish face.
Mouth and Teeth: Scissors mouth with inner surface of upper incisors playing upon the outer surface of lower incisors. Full complement of large, clean, ivory teeth, evenly spaced.	**Mouth and Teeth:** Mouth either undershot or pig-jawed. Either is a very bad fault. Teeth either too small, dirty or discolored or pitted, or diseased or decayed, or crooked.
Nose and Nostrils: Nose large and black, without flesh-colored spots; nostrils large, open, and active.	**Nose and Nostrils:** Flesh-colored or spotted nose; nostrils inadequately small.
Lips and Flews: Adequate only for squareness of muzzle.	**Lips and Flews:** "Dry" lips, inadequate for complete coverage of mouth and teeth and causing an appearance of snipiness. Lips too long and pendent.
Ears: Long and broad, reaching almost or quite to the nose when they are pulled forward. Soft and fine in texture, hanging flatly against the cheeks with only enough erectile power to give the face an alert expression. Natural and uncropped.	**Ears:** Short and narrow. Coarse or thick in texture. Too great an erectile power. Buttoned forward like the ears of an English Foxhound.

Look For:

Eyes: Of moderate size and as dark in color as is possible. (A lighter color, such as deep amber, permissible in eyes of a Hound with no other markings than tan on face and body. Even with tan markings, dark brown or black eyes are preferred.) Set well apart, but in the front of the brow. Neither so small as to appear porcine or stingy, nor so large and bulging as to seem Pug-like. The whites of the eyes well concealed by the lids. Eyes alert and placid with an expression of happiness and sweet nature.

Cheeks: Flat and without roundness or show of excess muscular development. Free from cheekiness.

Neck: Moderately long and very strong, sloping into well laid back shoulders. Moderately curved at its top (crested) somewhat more in the dog than in the bitch. Not exceedingly dry, but showing no surplus skin or dewlap at the throttle or under side of the neck.

Shoulders: Long and well laid back to high withers. Shoulder bones close together at their top. Approximately at right angles with upper arms. Flat and without muscular bulge on outside. Moderately tight, but free.

Avoid:

Eyes: Too small and pig-like, or too large and bulging. Any semblance of light-colored irises. Any show of the whites of the eyes. Any looseness or droop of the under lids. Set too close together or with a divergent look. Any absence of alertness in the expression. Any sourness or ill nature.

Cheeks: Bulging muscles over cheeks. Cheekiness.

Neck: Short, cloddy, or weak with upright shoulders. Stovepipe neck or ewe-neck (concave). Excess of skin under neck or throatiness.

Shoulders: Short and upright. Tops of shoulders spread far apart. Padded with surplus muscle. Loose or wobbly shoulders, or tight and constricted ones.

47

Look For:	Avoid:
Back and Body: Body short and compact without being cobby. Well sprung (but not rounded or barrel-shaped) ribs, extending downward at least as far as the elbows. Capacious chest. Ribs extended well back to short, strong, and muscular loin. Loin somewhat tucked up, but not excessively. Back line short and straight from withers to pelvis, lissome and flexible. Body well knit, muscular and hard.	**Back and Body:** Body long and/or slack. A narrow, flat rib-case, lacking capacity for heart and lungs. Shallow brisket. Ribs failing to extend well back. A long or weak loin. Loin without tuck-up, or with an excessive tuck-up such as that of Whippet. Back line long and slack. Sway-back or roachback Body muscles soft or pudgy.
Forelegs: Muscular with very heavy, hard bone. Dropping vertically from the elbows. Pastern joints quite straight and without "give." Moderately close together, but without semblance of a Terrier front.	**Forelegs:** Small or weak, soft bone. Insufficient muscle. Closer together at floor than at elbows or loosely sprawled and truss-fronted. Excessively narrow front.
Hindquarters and Rear Legs: Large, thick, wide and strong hams. Long thigh and stifle; short and vertical from hock joint to floor. Substantial bones. Considerable turn of stifle joint, but not so much angulation as to impair endurance.	**Hindquarters and Rear Legs.** Small, thin, narrow, or weak hams. Short thigh and/or stifle. Long hock or one angled forward to produce saber-hocks. Straight stifles to produce prop-like quarters, or their opposite, extreme turn of stifle and excessive angulation.
Feet: Short, round, thick, and well knuckled with toes compact, well knitted, and close together. Cat-like feet. Pads thick and tough. Nails short and heavy.	**Feet:** Long or thin, with toes open and splayed. Hare-feet. Thin, tender, or broken pads. Long, overgrown, or thin nails.
Tail or Stern: Strong and moderately short, set on rather high, moderately but not excessively curved, and carried high but short of the vertical, clothed with harsh, heavy brush.	**Tail or Stern:** Pipe-stopper, rat-like, or weak tail of too great length. Set on too low. Absolutely straight or curved forward enough to cut a line vertical to the point of insertion. Inadequately covered with hair or with soft hair.

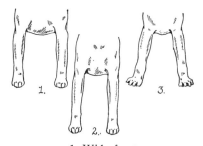

1. Wide front
2. Correct front
3. Narrow and splayed

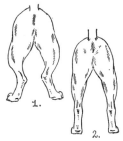

1. Cowhocks
2. Correct rear
3. Toed in

Look For:

Coat: A thick and dense covering of hard, straight, smooth hair, shortest on face, feet, and legs, somewhat longer on body, longest on neck, breech, and stern. The cross-section of the individual hair is thick. Hair is smooth, but springy to the touch. Coat for exhibition is natural and un-trimmed.

Action: True, sound, free, and straight forward. Feet turned directly toward the front. Hocks parallel. Shoulders open and legs free swinging. Rear legs demonstrating much power, drive, propulsion, and liberty. A jaunty gait, with tail in air, showing enthusiastic earnestness and happy good nature.

Avoid:

Coat: Soft, thin, or unhealthy. Too short or not adequately protective. Twisted like hair of a Wire-haired Fox Terrier. Coat trimmed or doctored.

Action: Crippled or awkward gait, or one lacking liberty. Feet turning inward (pigeon-toed) or turning outward (slue-footed). Either cow-hocks or bandy legs. Short and choppy steps. Weaving or paddling in front legs. Any show of weakness in the hindquarters or their use. Tail carried too low. Sourness of expression or of bearing. Viciousness or evil nature. Lack of enthusiasm.

49

In-Depth Study of the Standard

The Standard of the Beagle says the skull should be "fairly long." There is, however, no virtue in mere length. "Only moderately long" might have been better. Length may be accepted as in proportion to width, in which case the skull of the Beagle should not be long at all, for the Beagle does not have a "long, lean head;" the "cranium," according to the Standard, should be "broad and full." Neither is that intended to imply that the skull is as wide as possible, for it ought not to be. Again, "moderately" wide might better describe the skull of the Beagle. It must not be so wide as to appear coarse, since the Beagle is one of the most refined of dogs. There is nothing freakish about the breed. The skull is not flat, but rather slightly domed, there being a bit of curve both from side to side and from stop to occiput.

The muzzle is only slightly, if any, longer than the top-skull, full and broad, and neatly chiseled but not heavily cut away before the eyes. The lips or flews are deep and heavy enough to cover the teeth securely and to give the face a squarely truncated aspect. But they are not pendant or heavy. Flews that are too heavy drag upon the under lid of the eye and cause it to droop and show the haw. This mars the entire expression, giving the face the aspect of a Bloodhound. The stop is pronounced but not abrupt. The muzzle merges into the upper part of the head rather than appearing merely to be affixed to it.

The cheeks should be flat and without any bulge of muscles. Where such bulge is found, it is usually accompanied by muscular padding on the outside of the shoulders, an even worse fault than "cheekiness." This excessive development of the cheek muscles is frequently excused by an admiring owner by the statement that the dog as a puppy was permitted to gnaw bones or otherwise to exercise his jaws

Ch. King's Creek Triple Threat, 15", the greatest breed winning Beagle in history, appropriately pictured here scoring Best of Breed at the first annual specialty of the National Beagle Club, at the NBC's home—Institute Farm, Aldie, Va. in April, 1970. The entry totaled 128. "Trippe", co-owned by Lullaby Kennels and Tom Foy, Jr., was handled here by Marcia Foy. Judge, at left, was John P. Murphy, and club president Morgan Wing, Jr., presented the trophy. First shown in 1965, "Trippe" was one of the Top Ten Beagles for seven years, compiling a score of 347 Bests of Variety (believed a record for all breeds), 232 Group placements including 77 firsts, 8 all-breed Bests in Show and 3 Specialty Bests in Show.

too much. The assertion has no validity, for bulging cheek muscles are of genetic origin and no excessive use of the jaws can produce them unless the dog was endowed with them by his ancestors.

Whereas the official Standard of the Beagle defines the eyes as "large," they may easily be too large. They are only of medium size, which may be termed normal. The Standard should not be interpreted as implying that the Beagle should have pop-eyes. Excessively big eyes are prone to give a dog a toyish expression and, indeed, are frequently, but not always, found in smaller Beagles—those much less than thirteen inches at the shoulder.

While the Beagle's eyes should not be excessively large, an even worse fault in the breed is eyes excessively small, Terrier-like, sharp, or varminty. The eyes are "set well apart," the words of the Standard, but should be well within the borders of the cheeks. Certainly, there should be approximately the breadth of one eye between the eyes, which are well within the front of the face.

Beagle expression is determined largely by the size, shape, placement, and color of the eyes. That expression may well be defined as placid, soft, languishing, and exhibiting a will to please, but, in the healthy dog, alert and ready. The Standard declares that the eyes should be "of a brown or a hazel color;" as a matter of fact, they can hardly be too nearly black. A dark hazel eye is acceptable in a dog with exclusively tan markings around it, but even in such a dog, a brown eye approaching to black is to be preferred. An eye merely yellow or some other light color is much to be deplored in a Beagle.

A flesh-colored or unpigmented eye-rim, or an unpigmented spot of considerable size on an eye-rim, will mar an otherwise excellent expression on a Beagle. It is not mentioned in the Standard and, while not technically of great importance, such a "white" eye-rim will tend to prejudice a judge against the dog that has it.

The mouth of the Beagle is even, with a scissors bite. By "scissors bite" is meant such an occlusion of the jaws and

Ch. Validay Merrie Monarch, 15", Best of Breed at the second annual National Beagle Club specialty at Aldie, Va. in April, 1971. Owned by Validay Beagles, Reg. and handled by Bob Forsyth. William S. Houpt, left, was judge, and club president Morgan Wing, Jr., presented the trophy.

Ch. Wagon Wheels Wild Honey, owned by Miss Evelyn M. Droge, pictured winning the Best Brood Bitch award at the first annual National Beagle Club Specialty under judge John Murphy. The two bitches representing her get were Ch. Wagon Wheels Winter Holly, CD (center), and Ch. Wagon Wheels Dilly (right). Wild Honey, dam of nine champions, won the Best Brood Bitch award again at the second Specialty in 1971.

53

teeth that the upper incisors just play upon the lower ones and overlap them only so much that their inner surface just touches the outer surface of the lower incisors. An overshot upper jaw as well as an undershot lower one should be penalized, and the more exaggerated the deformation, the larger the penalty that is attached to it. One lifts the lips to examine the teeth, but this is a hardly necessary process to see faulty occlusion of the jaws. An overshot mouth will manifest itself exteriorly in a short and weak under jaw—what is called a fish-mouth or pig-jaw— which mars the expression of the whole face. On the other hand, an undershot mouth (evident from the exterior in a pugilistic, protruding lower jaw) gives the face a truculent, aggressive aspect, which is in conflict with the Beagle's placidity and kindly nature. The dental formation should include a full set of teeth, large, clean, white, and unbroken. Judges differ in their inclinations to penalize brown and pitted teeth, which result from some severe febrile disease, and are called "distemper teeth," but most good judges attach a large penalty to such a defect on the probably correct assumption that, while the distemper teeth are not directly inheritable, the predisposition for teeth to pit or rot from prolonged or high fever may be a genetic factor.

The nostrils of the Beagle are large and open, in keeping with the breed's function as a trailing Hound. Such nostrils are not only an aid to his ability to breathe deeply under exertion, but also offer a larger surface to his olfactory nerves. The nose is solid black in Beagles that have black anywhere in the coat marking. In dogs with tan markings only, a liver-colored nose may be acceptable, although even in them, black is preferred.

The face of the Beagle is framed by its ears, which in a great measure determine its expression. Those ears are large, both long and wide, low-set, pendant and almost lacking in erectile power. When they are drawn out, they extend well-nigh to the nose; at least, they cannot be too long, and their width will be in proportion. The ears do

Ch. Draper's Lemon Drop Daisy Mae, owned by Mrs. C. M. Draper and Mrs. John D. White, Jr., and handled by Mr. White, pictured winning the 13″ variety at the first annual National Beagle Club Specialty in 1970. Judge was John P. Murphy, and club vice-president David B. Sharp, Jr., presented the trophy. Daisy Mae was the top scoring 13″ Beagle in America for 1969.

Ch. Johjean Jubilation T. Cornbal, 15″, scoring Winners Dog as a puppy at the first annual National Beagle Club Specialty, Cornbal followed with wins of Best of Breed at the Southern California and Wisconsin Beagle Clubs' specialties. Owned by Jean H. Refieuna and Edward B. Jenner.

not hang directly downward, but rather over the cheek, pointed toward the throat. They do not wrinkle in the manner of the Bloodhound. Their erectile muscles are almost nonexistent, and the ears lift only slightly in the display of animation. The leather of the ears is thin, soft, and flexible.

The description of the ears in the official Standard of the Beagle declares that they are "rounded at the tip." This is an unfortunate and misleading phrase, for the ears of the Beagle are not and never should be surgically "rounded" in the manner of the English Foxhound. It only means they are naturally (not artificially) round rather than pointed.

The Beagle neck is long and strong. When we say it is long, we do not imply that it is swan-like, but a short neck betrays an upright shoulder, which is one of the worst faults a Beagle may possess. The neck is at least long enough that the Hound is able to take food from the floor without spreading or trussing its front legs. And the neck must be powerful enough, and to spare, to enable the Hound easily to lift a large hare from the ground. The top line of the neck is marked by a crest, somewhat higher and more curved in the dog than in the bitch, but it is never stove-pipe straight. The worst possible neck is one with a concave top line—an ewe-neck as it is called because of its supposed resemblance to the neck of a female sheep. Such a neck betrays weakness. The neck is more than a mere connection between the Hound's body and head. It is a flexible, supple, and strong anatomical part by means of which the head is manipulated, carried, raised, lowered, and turned. The power for this activity is best attained by a neck that is large and substantial at the base and tapering as it rises gracefully toward the high head, proudly carried.

The Beagle's throat is clean and without surplus skin. This must not be taken to imply that the skin must be so "dry" and close fitting as that, for instance, of the Doberman Pinscher. It is comfortably loose, as is the skin over the rest of the body. But the throat must show no dewlap

Ch. Page Mill Wildfire, 13″, a top winner of the mid-60s. Bred by A. D. and C. Gordon, and owned by Dr. and Mrs. A. C. Musladin.

Ch. Validay Jupiter, 13″, by Int. Ch. Opus Tubac Trumpeter ex Ch. Validay Courtly, and owned by Validay Beagles, Reg.

like the throat of the Bloodhound, and, indeed, no throatiness. The Standard says, "slight wrinkle below the angle
of the jaw, however, may be allowed," but we may add
that the smaller such wrinkle be, if there be one, the
better.

This strong neck, such as is described, fits neatly into
and between the long, sloping, and well laid back shoulders. Perfect shoulders are seldom found on a Beagle, but
it is of utmost importance that they shall be at least adequate. The shoulder blades are long, their upper ends having but little space between them and forming a high
wither. They are, as nearly as possible, at a right angle with
the long bone of the upper arm, the humerus. Any tendency to an uprightness of the shoulder blades is a fault
that cannot be easily forgiven. The shoulders are flat, without evidence of short, bunched, or bulging muscles over
them.

The back from withers to pelvis is short and absolutely
straight and level. In so saying, distinction must be made
between length of back and length of Hound over all. An
animal with adequate forechest and large, strong hams
may be as long as it may, provided that its length is not
achieved by any prolongation of the length of its back
from withers to pelvis. The power of locomotion in any
quadruped is developed in the hindquarters and transmitted through the back to the shoulders and forequarters.
It is therefore essential that the back shall be short, that
no part of that transmitted power be lost or dissipated in
the process.

It is equally important that the back be quite level. Any
roach or hump of the back implies constriction of the
muscles, and any sag or sway of the back indicates a loss
of power and energy.

The croup, which is the continuation of the back line
beyond the junction with the pelvis, shows a just percep-
tible slope downward. A high-carried tail with a low set-on
is awkward and looks somewhat like a handle on a teapot;

Ch. Validay Electric Ember, 15″, by Jubilee Gay Cinder ex Validay Tempest. Owned by Validay Beagles, Reg.

Ch. Herold's Prince Charles, 15″, by Ch. Johnson's Fancy Boots ex Lady Alexandra of Nutley. Owned by Validay Beagles, Reg.

and a set-on of tail on an absolutely level croup is likely to throw the tail too far forward and over the back. The Beagle's tail or brush should be carried gaily and high, but not quite vertically from the back and never so far forward as to lean toward the front.

The Beagle is well ribbed out and well ribbed back, giving it as large a thoracic cavity to accommodate a big heart and spacious lungs as is compatible with the individual Hound's overall size. The back is broad, the ribs springing wide from the spine but reaching their maximum expanse at the top. Thence they round very gently in their descent to the brisket. They are capacious and yet rather flat on the sides. Barrel-shaped ribs are admired only by the uninformed, for such ribs interfere with the elbows and impede the action of the forelegs.

The brisket, on an adult Beagle, extends downward at least as far as the elbow, and it is desirable if it reaches somewhat below that point. It is safe to say that the deeper the rib-case, the better, and horizontally, the longer, the better. The length of the body is occupied largely by the length of the rib-case.

The loin is accordingly short. It is, however, of considerable depth, the muscles hard and exceedingly strong. There is some, but little tuck-up of the abdomen, enough to save the Hound from any aspect of being "sausage bodied." The moderation in this tuck-up denotes strength and endurance rather than speed.

From the elbows, the front legs drop plummet-like and absolutely straight to the feet. It is in these features that faults may be frequently found in many Beagles. There should be no evidence of pastern joints in the standing Beagle. The size of the leg should not shrink below that point, and there should be no give to the pastern joint nor should the pastern "knuckle over" or bulge forward. In an excess of zeal for straightness of pastern, too many breeders have encouraged Hounds that show the opposite of soft pasterns and accordingly there is a forward turn at that joint which should not be there.

60

Ch. Little Giant of Park Lane, 13″, Best of Variety at Westminster 1964, and at International, Beverly Hills and Santa Barbara —the nation's three largest shows —in 1965. Handled by owner Alice Jeffrey.

Am. & Can. Ch. Socum Tammy, 13″, pictured winning the variety at Westminster in 1961. Ten years later, Tammy was still active hunting rabbits. One of the top producing bitches of all time, Tammy produced champions in six litters, bred to a different dog each time. On top of a great show record, she topped a Sanction Field Trial, scoring over four field champions. Co-owned by Jean H. Refieuna and Edward B. Jenner. (Handled in photo by Dick Cooper).

Ch. Gay Boy of Geddesburg, 15″, the top winning Beagle in America for 1961 and 1962. In those two years alone, Gay Boy scored 9 Bests in Show and 51 Group Firsts. Owned by Mr. and Mrs. Willard K. Denton.

Ch. Hi Spirit Jay, a top 15″ winner of the mid-60s, with an overall score of 126 Bests of Variety, 20 Group firsts, 3 all-breed Bests in Show and 4 Specialties. Owned by Mr. and Mrs. Tom Foy, Jr.

It has already been said that the leg is absolutely straight from the elbow to the foot. This requires emphasis, since an outward curvature of the bones of the lower leg is too frequently encountered in Beagles and is very reprehensible when it is found. These bowed legs are not to be confused with trussed legs, in which the feet are farther apart than the elbows, an equally faulty front formation, about which more will be said in those paragraphs of this chapter which treat of gait and action, in which the trussed legs reflect themselves.

The feet should be short, round, small, and cat-like, with rugged, substantial nails, worn down short. The pad (what the English Foxhound Standard calls the "horn") is thick and tough for long usage over rough or rocky terrain without crippling injury. The feet point directly forward; any turning in or out is to be avoided.

The correct front, here described, should be neither narrow nor wide, neither so narrow as that of the Greyhound nor so wide as that of the Dachshund. There must be room enough between the legs to accommodate a capacious chest and brisket, the capacity of which is attained rather by depth than width.

The hindquarters are both wide and thick with generous musculature of hams and buttocks. The Beagle is to be followed by the huntsmen on foot, and there is therefore no requirement for excessive angulation. This is not to say that the hindquarters of the Beagle are straight—mere props. The propulsive power of the dog is developed in the hindquarters through the leverage of its parts and there must be adequate turns of stifle and hock to propel the Hound over the ground. The staying power, indefatigability, however, is more important than speed.

The thigh and second-thigh are both long, and the hock well let down and short. The hindquarters are fore-square; the hind feet pointed directly forward, turned neither in nor out; the hocks quite upright, perpendicular to the floor when the Hound is not in motion; and the hocks showing no tendency to converge. The hindquarters, like the forequarters, are substantial, with the large bones clothed with powerful muscles, which provide sustained driving power.

Even the tail or brush is large and powerful, not excessively long but never docked. It is set on moderately high, but not absolutely on top of the back, and carried in a slight, graceful curve, short of the vertical.

The coat of the Beagle is moderately long but smooth and flat. The individual hairs are heavy and straight. There is no pile or undercoat. The coat on the head, ears, and front of legs is short, with a longer frill on the neck, back of the legs, and tail. In preparing a Beagle for exhibition the coat is never trimmed or shortened, although the vibrissae (the coarse, long hairs on the muzzle and over the eyes, sometimes known as the "feelers") may be shortened.

Color may be said to be immaterial. The Standard of the breed specifies "any true Hound color." The recognized Hound colors are black, tan, or black-and-tan, on a white ground, although gray, brindle, or grizzle are acceptable. While not required, symmetrical markings on the head are attractive, and a Hound suffers in general appearance unless its head markings are approximately regular.

Now, it should be asked if the structure of the animal in standing position appears to be satisfactory; then the Hound should be moved by his handler so that his "manner of going" may be examined. However well made a Beagle may appear to be, if he fails in his action he is useless. It is an old axiom among dog fanciers that "gait is the test of structure," but the converse that structure is the test of gait is equally true. Structure and gait are so closely interrelated that the animal that is made right cannot move wrong. Nevertheless, some fault in the structure that may be overlooked in the standing examination is sure to be evident in the Beagle in action.

The handler should lead the Hound first away from and then back toward the examiner at a slow walk, afterward at a trot. This may be repeated once or several times until the examiner is satisfied.

Ch. The Whim's Buckeye, top 13″ Beagle of 1970. A Group and Best in Show winner. Owned by Dr. and Mrs. A. C. Musladin.

Ch. The Whim's Butler Bugle, 13″ bitch, twice winner of the breed at Blossom Valley Beagle Specialty, and twice Best of Variety at Southern California Specialty. Owned by Dr. and Mrs. A. C. Musladin.

The Hound should move with all feet pointing directly forward. There should be no hitch in the hind legs, and no spraddle. The hocks should not be so close together as to threaten to interfere with each other or to leave an impression of three point suspension. Neither should they be so far apart as to cause the rump to waddle in its shift from one side to the other. The hocks should move forward in parallel planes, and should converge at their tops no more in moving than in standing. Cowhocks, as such convergence is called, which may not be noticed in the standing animal are instantly apparent when the animal moves away from the examiner. And they are unforgiveable in any sporting dog such as the Beagle.

Looked at from the side in action, the back should appear level, as it should in standing. It is not absolutely stiff, but free and flexible.

As the Hound returns toward the examiner, the front legs are seen to swing in parallel planes, the feet entirely and cleanly clearing the ground but with no semblance of the lost motion of high or hackney action. Such action is often overlooked or forgiven, sometimes it is admired and applauded, but it is wrong. The energy wasted in excessive raising of the feet and waving them in the air could better be used in propelling the Beagle over the ground.

Nor should the front feet cross each other and weave, the result of too loose an attachment of the shoulders. Neither should they paddle in action, the feet throwing alternately to the side. This results from too tight an attachment of the shoulders.

Overall Beagle action should be free, powerful, effortless; the steps long, springy, and flexible. Such a Hound is said to have liberty, which is as great praise as one can bestow.

The Beagle is indeed a dog, but among hunting people he is never so spoken of, except the male Beagle to distinguish him from the bitch. The Beagle is a *Hound* and properly so designated. He should be so called and so judged. Incidentally, the Beagle male dog employed for breeding is not a mere stud-dog. By Hound people he is known as a *stallion,* and he should look like one.

66

Ch. End O'Maine Ridge Runner, 15", the top winning show Beagle of the mid-50s. Owned by Philip B. Jacobi, he was bred and handled by Hollis Wilson, today a respected all-breed judge.

A current winner, Ch. Colegren's Flaming Ochre, 15", finished to championship in two months with four majors. Bred by Wm. L. Coleman and handled by Jane F. Kamp.

Ch. Wagon Wheels Winter Sport, 15", sire of 18 champions. Bred and owned by Miss Evelyn M. Droge, and handled by Damara Bolte.

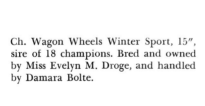

67

SOUND ADVICE

If you are feeling blue, old man,
And your spirit is getting down
My advice to you is this,
Get yourself a beagle hound.

Then when you come home at night,
He will wag his tail in greeting,
The things that he would like to say
Are well worth while repeating.

And though he really cannot talk,
He knows when things are amiss,
If he could but speak the words,
They probably would sound like this.

"Please don't feel so blue, old man,
I know you are tired and weary,
Take me out to the woods tonight,
And I will try to make it cheery.

"Let's go down to the old brush lot,
Where the rabbits romp and play,
And there I will do my best
To drive your blues away."

And so you take your little friend,
Off to the woods you go,
He trotting so merrily ahead,
You trudging behind so slow.

At last you reach the wooded spot
And "Pal" starts nosing around,
He soon will have a bunny up,
You can tell just by the sound.

At first it may only be a squeal,
But I'm sure it won't be long,
Before he opens loud and clear
With that merry beagle song.

Colegren Beagles

He'll drive that bunny far and wide
At a fast and furious pace,
For he wants to cheer his master,
With this hard and thrilling chase.

If red blood courses through your veins,
You'll forget your world's cares,
For this is just the sort of chase
That answers a beagler's prayers.

Your face will lose that constant frown,
You replace it with a smile,
And when this thrilling hunt is o'er,
Life again will seem worth while.

I see a new gleam in your eye,
As down to "Pal" you bend,
And the merry little beagle
Has made another lifelong friend.

You ask me how I know all this?
And why I give this advice so free?
Well, this same thing happened to someone else,
And that someone else was——ME.

Henry J. Colombo.

Justifiably Proud

Sketch by Paul Brown, courtesy Gaines Dog Research Center

The Gun Beagle

By Lew Madden

AS a gun dog and hunting companion the Beagle ranks supreme and during the course of any open gunning season probably has more shots fired over him than all other breeds of sporting dogs combined.

Rabbit hunting is, beyond question, the most universally accepted sport of our nation's nimrods, young and old alike. The cottontail abounds everywhere and is apparently affected less by the inroads of civilization than any other game animal. Youthful hunters cut their eye teeth and old timers round out their hunting careers in quest of him. The Beagle is his counterpart and where you find the cottontail you will find the Beagle right there in pursuit of him.

Gunning plays a very important role on the American scene. It is a heritage passed down to us from our pioneer ancestors who had to be proficient at it in order to survive. We have never been able to get it out of our system and let's hope we never do. In spite of man's interferences such as rural developments, modern methods of farming, strip mining, pesticides, pollution, etc., a bountiful Mother Nature still continues to provide a plentiful supply of game that naturalists and other wildlife authorities tell us should be harvested to prevent overpopulation which in turn would lead to starvation, disease or an overpopulation of predators. Authoritative studies on the effects of heavy gunning pressure in good rabbit cover have disclosed that removal of up to 75% of the bunnies had no effect on the number available the following season. Therefore, the blasphemous remarks sometimes hurled at gunners by those who are averse to killing are for the most part, unfounded. Nature's methods of disposing of her surplus populations are much less merciful than man's methods of harvesting them.

The skilled rabbit hunter with his well trained Beagle causes little suffering to the game he seeks. His respect for the skill and capability of his hound will prompt him to shoot only when there is certainty of a clean and merciful kill. He does not have reason to take pot shots in uncertain situations because he knows his hound will give him another opportunity and he has no fear of not filling his game bag, if that be his goal. The proficiency of the Beagle to find, pursue, and drive his quarry into range of his master's gun insures the success of the hunt and even on occasions when the game bag may not be filled to the desirable level the memories of the hound's accomplishments will long be cherished by his owner.

Small in stature, but stout of heart, the Beagle's size and intestinal fortitude fit him almost beyond description to perform the duties and overcome the obstacles that he must face during the course of the day's hunt. His size makes it possible for him to explore even the sometimes almost impenetrable cover his quarry is capable of hiding in. His determined and relentless manner of pursuing his game, his uncanny skill at solving the many intricate puzzles his quarry is capable of presenting, the tremendous amount of stamina that he has wrapped up in his tough little hide and the gay manner in which he goes about his work as though he enjoyed it even during the late hours of the hunt—when tired, torn and weary his devotion to duty prompts him to scorn fatigue—makes him a cherished addition to any hunting party. When you put your shotgun on your shoulder and unsnap his leash, his attitude immediately becomes one of "be my guest" and he makes you feel as though you were being entertained by a gracious and capable host.

The gun Beagle could very well be termed the "work horse" of the breed. Unquestionably he is the greatest press agent it could have. He may not be registered or pedigreed. In fact, he may not even be full blooded but if he is a good rabbit dog, that part of him which is Beagle gets the credit. By word of mouth, rather than through the power of the press, his worthiness in the hunting field is legend, and if by chance all organized efforts to promote the breed should cease, the breed itself would be sustained through the gun dog. In sections of the country where no clubs exist and where shows and field trials are unheard of, you will find that the gun Beagle is a very common sight and a survey of the back yards of any community will astound you by the esteem in which he is held.

Training the gun Beagle is a very simple task, and the breed itself might very well be classified as "born trained." Few, and quite possibly no other breeds of dog, have the natural aptitude to take to their work as does the Beagle. His inquisitive nature, even during the early stages of puppyhood, causes him to explore and seek enjoyment in locating the causes of the many tantalizing odors that his sensitive little nose reveal. His friendly nature and love for human companionship makes him tractable and easy to control and his inherent trailing ability, handed down through many generations of capable ancestors, provides him with the ability quickly to grasp the purpose for which he was created. As a puppy, he comes endowed with all the necessary talents to serve his hunting master, and all he needs to become a skilled artist is an opportunity to learn his trade.

Many of the best gun dogs are developed by giving them free range and permitting them to self hunt. Quite often dogs trained in this manner are, at least at first, hard to control and keep within range of the hunt, but if the hunter is not a stickler for control and obedience he will find that the added experience of such hounds will more than offset their unwillingness to obey. With a little patience hounds trained in this manner soon learn to be a part of the team and develop

73

a love for behaving in a manner that will draw praise from their masters. Contrary to many opinions, hunting dogs are not spoiled by making pets of them. Human companionship, the more the better, is the best way to develop an understanding between the hunter and his dog. Your secret of success in bagging game will not be based on how good a shot you are or how perfect a dog you have but on how good a team you make. By association, you will learn to know your dog, good points and bad, and he will learn to know and understand you and your teamwork will pay off.

For the owner who prefers to "train" his dog himself, developing control and obedience as the hound learns to hunt, there are no secret methods. Simply get him out where he can find game to run and he will do the rest. Always be where he expects you to be, never fool him, don't expect the impossible from him and don't oversupervise him, but let him learn to rely on his own initiative. This will give him confidence in you as well as in his own ability and once he has this self-assurance you will be surprised at his progress. Praise for his accomplishments will spur him on in his efforts to please you, and a scolding will often suffice to discourage him from doing things you disapprove. Sterner methods are sometimes necessary with obstinate individuals but once your hound has respect for you, he will refrain from doing the things you disapprove to a great extent. Treat him like a partner and let him understand that you and he are both in the same business and you will never have to worry about him not doing more than his share to make every hunt an enjoyable one.

The novice hunter is likely to face the purchase of his first Beagle with a feeling of mixed emotions. At the same time that he is experiencing the joyful anticipation of possessing a capable hunting partner he is filled with the fear that his hound may not come up to his expectations. Such faults as gun-shyness, lack of desire to search, failure to stick or unwillingness to keep within the range of the hunt, render a dog valueless to the hunter. If the purchaser is buying a trained gun dog he should check for these faults before making any deal. The best place to make the purchase is from a local

74

Beagler or hunter who is known to be reliable and has a reputation for keeping good hounds. Then ask him to take the dog out and give you a demonstration of its abilities. In this manner you will see your prospect under normal conditions in familiar company for the type of hunting cover you will expect to use him in, and if price is an object with you, the money you save on transportation costs can be applied toward a better specimen.

If you purchase a puppy, purchase locally if you can find a reliable breeder nearby. If you are sure your puppy comes from good stock, you can discard your worries about how he is likely to turn out, to a great extent. Contrary to some opinions, I am convinced that no dog is born gunshy. Some strains may be of a more nervous temperament than others which would naturally render them more susceptible to sudden unexpected noises. If you analyze your dog properly and don't frighten him by shooting when he is unprepared or not interested in game, he will soon learn to associate the crack of the gun with pleasure and come to love it. After a few rabbits have been shot ahead of him and he is allowed to come to them and possibly be rewarded with some blood or liver he will hark to the crack of the gun just as quickly as to another hound giving tongue.

To encourage your dog to search, first go with him into the coverts where game is likely to be found and if necessary, jump his first few rabbits for him. Once he has become aware that game exists in the area, refrain as much as possible from helping him locate it. If you become the jumper, he is quite likely to get the impression that that is your job and depend on you to do it to a great extent. By making him find his own game he will soon learn to assume this responsibility and become adept at it, and will save you many unnecessary steps and scratches when on a hunting expedition. Searching comes naturally with most Beagles, but searching ability is only arrived at through experience.

Failure to stick at those long hard losses is quite often the fault of the master, rather than the dog. In primary training, the first thing the hunter should do is give his hound the assurance that he will not leave him. Young hounds sometimes become concerned about the whereabouts of their master and if they have been out of contact for some time, especially on a long loss, may check back to see if you are still there. Always be there when your hound returns and when he has located you, take him back to where he lost and encourage him to regain the trail, but don't under any circumstances interfere with him while he is working and don't give him help when there is a chance that he may be able to solve the problem himself. Every piece of game he jumps and every obstacle he overcomes on his own will be an incentive for him to go on to greater accomplishments until eventually you will find yourself possessed of a gun dog that makes you the envy of all your hunting companions.

Although the main usage of the gun Beagle is in hunting rabbits, he is quite capable of handling many other types of game, such as hare, fox, pheasant, deer, etc. He is very adaptable and wherever you live, or whatever kind of game abounds in your locality as long as it leaves a trail to follow, he will give it a try.

The size of the Beagle you choose for your gunning purposes should depend on the type of game you wish to hunt, the ruggedness of the terrain, the density of the cover and the range of distance the quarry travels when pursued. Small hounds can operate best in dense cover whereas larger hounds have the advantage in bigger country or on longer running quarries where stamina is of prime importance. The small Beagle is very adept at routing game from heavy brush piles and brambles which the larger hounds have trouble penetrating, as well as being very competent in following game that resorts to trickery rather than speed. On the other hand the large hound has the advantage of moving game that chooses to run in the open at a much faster pace and bring it back into shooting range much quicker than would his smaller counterpart in the same situation.

The Beagle is hunted in many manners, according to the whims of his owners. When hunted single he must be independent enough to stay out there on the job alone and resourceful enough to overcome the obstacles he will encounter without help. When hunted in a brace or pack, he must be cooperative enough to work harmoniously with other hounds contributing his share but not interfering with the work of his companions. He must display independence to the extent that he is not influenced by the faulty actions of other hounds, yet be willing to hark in to them to help them move the quarry when they are making progress. The proper methods of doing this are explained elsewhere in this book in the description of the "Field Trial Beagle."

The duties of the gun Beagle are few: three, to be exact. First, he must locate game. Second, he must pursue it until shot or holed. Third, he must hunt with his master. The main requirements are: first, an intense desire to hunt, second, a strong determination to stick, third, the stamina necessary to go all day or as long as his master wishes to hunt, and fourth, he must not run trash or off game. The characteristics necessary to accomplish the above purposes and perform the above duties are, a keen nose with which to trail, an intelligent brain to control the actions and overcome the problems, and a strong body to avoid undue fatigue.

If a dog has these characteristics and requirements and performs these duties, he is a good gun dog and is a valuable asset as a hunting companion. His owner need not be as critical of the methods his hound uses in performing his duties as must the field trial Beagler, but you can bet your bottom dollar that he will insist that they are performed, and that results are obtained.

The good field trial Beagle will make the best gun dog. If he has the previously mentioned requirements in addition to those necessary to put on a good field trial performance the gunner will be treated to the added features of listening to steadier runs and observing more accurate hound work.

Yes, the gun Beagle is a very valuable asset to the breed. He maintains its popularity in sections of the country where no organized efforts to popularize it exists and by so doing, eventually leads many of his admirers into the field of organized Beagling.

In the fall, his joyous cry can be heard everywhere as he routs and drives his game to his master's gun, and he is KING.

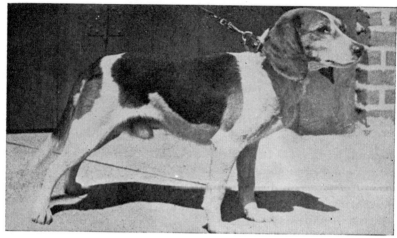

FIELD CHAMPION HARWOOD'S SPORT FLASH
February 15, 1933—November 6, 1944

Owned by Richardson Harwood, Natick, Massachusetts, "Sport," truly one of the great Hounds, was said by many to be the most sensational Beagle ever seen at the trials. An odd characteristic was the manner of carrying his tail low, as shown here, and even when running a rabbit, his tail had a low sweeping action.

The Field Trial Beagle

By Lew Madden

THE Beagle is a trailing hound whose purpose is to find game and pursue it in an energetic and decisive manner. To do this he must possess a keen nose, a strong desire to hunt, a determination to stick, a sturdy body and an intelligent mind.

Beagle field trials are held for the purpose of selecting those outstanding individuals that possess the above qualities and characteristics to the greatest degree and that display them to the best advantage in the most positive manner. Actions which indicate that any of the above qualities or characteristics are lacking to any degree are considered cause for demerit, and the penalty imposed is in proportion to the extent that they interfere with or fail to contribute to the efficient accomplishment of a desirable performance.

Winners are selected by comparing their performance against that of their competitors, rather than against a standard of perfection. A primary or first series is run to select those individuals who by their accomplishments indicate they are worthy of further consideration. These selected individuals are then required to run against each other, as directed by the judges, until eventually the winner and all place hounds have defeated their nearest rival in direct competition.

79

To be a successful competitor, in addition to the qualifications mentioned before, the Field Trial Beagle must be relatively free of faults, especially those which interfere with or prevent a steady progressive performance. These faults are also cause for demerit to whatever extent they interfere with accomplishment. Mere lack of fault is not cause for merit and the hound with minor faults that accomplishes much is preferred to the nearly flawless performer who accomplishes much less.

Years ago, some wise old hound man advised "look for perfection, but don't expect to find it." Experienced hound men agree unanimously that the perfect hound has never been born and is not likely to be. Realizing this and the difficulty in following by scent a quarry skilled in the art of eluding pursuit, over terrain that presents a variation of scenting conditions, man settles for the next best thing, which is a minimum of imperfection. He tries to eliminate faults in his hounds by judicious breeding and proper training. He tests his progress by entering his hounds in field trials to compare their quality against that of dogs developed by other breeders. In so doing he pits his breeding skill, his choice of bloodlines and his training methods against those of his fellow Beaglers in open competition under competent judges. By comparison, the judges decide which hound performs best under existing conditions on that particular occasion. In this manner Beagle breeders keep themselves informed of the progress being made by their fellow men, and of the hound characteristics predominating in various bloodlines or blends of bloodlines. They are thereby able to avail themselves of the benefit other bloodlines might offer to their own strains.

The purpose of holding field trials is to display talent and uncover faults in the contestants so that the knowledge gained can be used as a guide in producing better hounds. By recognizing mistakes and striving for perfection Beaglers hope to upgrade the quality of their hounds.

The ideal field trial Beagle is a remarkable specimen. He must be diligent at all times when afield, both in searching for game and when attempting to recover losses. He must remain as close to the line as possible because the scent of the trial is his only link with his quarry. He must be accurate in his work to avoid prolonged interruptions in the chase and he must claim his progress in a positive manner and remain silent when not making progress. His work will be carefully scrutinized by competent judges who will be looking for a display of talent with positive, accurate perseverance and a minimum of fault. The hounds that deliver this kind of performance with regularity are chosen by discriminating breeders to influence future generations.

Today, breeders give little consideration to the hound that cannot complete his "Field Trial Championship." Consequently few hounds that have not won this honor get their names in many pedigrees. Becoming a field champion is no easy task. It requires at least three first place wins and a total of 120 points to become a champion. Points are given according to the number of starters in any class. For each starter, the first place hound gets one point; second place hound gets ½ point; third place hound ⅓ point; and the fourth place hound gets ¼ of a point. A hound may be lucky enough to win or place occasionally without being exceptionally talented but it is unlikely that luck alone could secure his championship in today's stiff competition.

By using field trials as a testing ground and the most successful performers as breeding stock, the wise breeder often succeeds in building a strain of uniform, talented hounds capable of winning themselves and of passing their desirable traits on to their progeny. Several popular sires, produced by mating only the best to the best, have in recent years produced over 100 offspring each that have won their titles, and several famous bitches have produced 6 to 11, champions each.

The effects of upgrading the quality of the field trial Beagle are far-reaching. Since the field trial patron must retain only the best specimens in his kennel if he is to win, he has many better than average hounds to dispose of, usually to gunners. These hounds in most cases are just as good for gunning purposes as the best field trial hound could be, lacking only the extra margin of excellence it takes to win trials. Thus, the gun hound is upgraded right along with the field trial

81

Beagle in a manner impossible without the organized methods of testing quality afforded by holding field trials.

Any one interested in participating in field trials should get a copy of the "Beagle Field Trial Rules and Standard Procedures" and study it thoroughly. This book can be obtained free of charge from the American Kennel Club, 51 Madison Ave., New York, N.Y. 10010. It is invaluable for teaching the principles by which organized events are conducted and for describing the points of merit and demerit completely. Judges are required to know and judge by the rules and procedures set forth in this book. The Beagler should learn from the governing body how his hound is expected to perform if he is to win.

The Field Trial Beagler

By Lew Madden

THE group known as Field Trial Bea-
glers has done more to promote the breed to its present
popularity than all other groups combined. Superb organization by dedicated Beaglers has resulted in the sport of
Field Trial Beagling being closely knitted together, despite
its farflung scope.

Combining such facilities as the American Kennel Club,
which governs breed activities wisely and justly, and *Hounds
and Hunting* magazine, the largest single breed publication
in existence, which promotes the breed zealously and publi-
cizes it widely, with the many clubs, associations and feder-
ations whose purpose is to sponsor and conduct events in an
orderly and businesslike manner, the organization-minded
Beagler has, through sheer dedication to the sport and breed,
parlayed it from relative nonenity to almost unbelievable
popularity in the short span of years since the first field trial
was held at Hyannis, Massachusetts, in 1890.

Figures received from the American Kennel Club disclosed
that a total of 415 Beagle clubs have been recommended by
the Beagle Advisory Committee to conduct licensed field
trials during the season of July 1, 1965 through June 30, 1966.
Of these 415 field trials, 347 will be run in braces on rabbits

(B.R.), 40 will be run in large packs on hare (L.P.H.), 27 will be run in small packs on rabbits (S.P.R.), and one trial will be run in small packs on hare (S.P.H.). Unlike the early days of Beagling when field trial activities were confined to a few autumn months, events are now held throughout the entire year, and many States which in the past had frowned on any field activities during the small game breeding season have revised their laws now to permit trials to be held during this time.

The Field Trial Beagler's slogan of "Enjoy the chase, rather than the Kill," and his willingness to go "all out" to conserve and protect the game that furnishes him sport has earned him the respect of game conservationists, who look upon him as an asset, rather than a liability to their cause. In the same manner, his conduct when afield and his attitude towards the property of landowners upon which he runs makes him a good neighbor and welcome guest. Realization that he is a guest more often than a host prompts him to act with consideration in order to remain in the good graces of those who permit him to run over their lands, a privilege without which he could not function.

In the early stages of the sport field trials were sometimes conducted under rather primitive conditions. An old barn or abandoned house, if available, served as a headquarters. Lunches, mostly sandwiches and pop, were often dispensed from a tent and field trial grounds were anywhere that rabbits might be found. A couple of judges on foot, who in many cases made up their own rules as they went along, a marshal, a few brush beaters and some hounds, and you were in business.

Today's modern field trial presents a very different picture. Most present day Beagle clubs either own or lease the grounds upon which they run. Many of these grounds are enclosed with rabbit-proof fence to keep the game available as well as to furnish protection for the hounds from highway hazards or the possibility of getting out of the country in pursuit of a deer or fox. Club houses are in most cases as modern as the average home with all of the facilities for preparing savory meals and providing necessary comforts.

84

The present day Beagler quite often is accompanied by his entire family who enjoy themselves in pleasant surroundings and company. Judges are generally mounted and operate in accordance to a strict set of rules which they are required to know, and the entries are quite numerous, often totaling more than 100 in a class. Game, by good management, is generally kept available in sufficient quantity to permit events even of unexpected size to be conducted on a scheduled basis.

This great sport of Field Trial Beagling, once so rugged as to be limited to the hardy outdoorsman, has now been so refined that it is fast becoming the hobby of his family. Wife, mother, son, daughter, sweetheart, and even baby are all welcome guests to be taken along when daddy goes out to enjoy his sport and the friendships made are invariably of lasting duration.

Beagle field trials, once comparatively rare and confined to a few sections of the country, are now spreading to all parts of the Nation and Canada. Anyone interested in locating an established club can do so by contacting *Hounds and Hunting* magazine, Bradford, Pennsylvania. If no club exists in your area and you are desirous of forming one *Hounds and Hunting* will be glad to publicize your intention so that it may be seen by others who might also be interested. Don't hesitate to join this fast growing sport. It can give you untold enjoyment by providing healthful recreation as well as creating lasting friendships.

Turning Sharp On Line

Sketch by Paul Brown, courtesy Gaines Dog Research Center

Cottontail Field Trials

By Henry J. Colombo

SINCE that memorable day, November 4, 1890, when at Hyannis, Massachusetts, the National Beagle Club held the first cottontail field trial ever to be run in the world, the wonderful sport of field trials for Beagles, both on cottontail and hare, has grown to an immensity that surely would astound even the most optimistic of those early pioneering Beaglers. There was a grand total of eighteen entries at that first trial. Today, it is not uncommon to see entries exceeding two hundred at a single trial.

In 1893, the New England Beagle Club at Oxford, Massachusetts, and the Northwestern Beagle Club at Whitewater, Wisconsin, became the second and third clubs to conduct field trials for Beagles. The National and the New England have continued to be active to this day and are holding field trials regularly.

The early growth of Beagle field trials was very slow, there still being only three held in 1900. The number grew to five in 1910 and to seventeen by 1919. In 1940, just fifty years after the birth of the Beagle field trial, the number of trials licensed by the American Kennel Club had reached fifty-three. Many of the old-time conservatives felt that the field trial sport was now growing too fast for its own good. How mistaken they were. The merry little Beagle

87

FIELD CHAMPION GRAY'S LINESMAN
May 28, 1936—June 19, 1950
This is a heretofore unpublished photograph of the Beagle world's leading pro-
ducing sire of field champions—over 60 of his get have acquired the title.

was becoming more popular every day. Increasing numbers of men, boys, and women, too, were being bitten by the field trial bug as I had been after attending my first trial in the spring of 1934. Rabbit hunters were becoming Beaglers. What a thrill to put your Hound down in friendly competition against your neighbor, friend, or total stranger, but all sportsmen. Licensed trials were increasingly rapidly, advancing to 110 in 1945, 205 in 1950, and 294 in 1954. In 1964, the A.K.C. reported 54,619 dogs which competed at 403 field trials located in 35 states. Pennsylvania led the states with 61 trials in which there were 10,273 competing entries, surely proof of the phenomenal popularity of the Beagle and modern Beagling.

All prospective Beaglers should affiliate with a Beagle club. Organized Beagling is much more fun than hunting alone or without benefit of the experience of others who have studied the breed and the sport. Many prospective Beaglers probably hesitate to participate in organized competition because they fear their efforts will not measure up to those of the more experienced and that their amateurish actions will be noticed and criticized by the more proficient. Such is not the case. Many of the experienced Beaglers, remembering their greenhorn days, willingly assist the novice. It is easy for Beaglers to meet on an even keel, for they have a common interest and speak the same language.

Field Championship points are awarded only at Member (A.K.C. member clubs) Field Trials or Licensed (non-member) Field Trials, and on the following basis: 1 point to the winner of first place for each Hound started; ½ point to second place; ⅓ point to third place; and ¼ point to fourth place. (Example: 40 Hounds in class. 40 points to first place; 20 points to second; 13⅓ points to third; and 10 points to fourth.) The total number of points necessary for a Beagle to win in order to be declared a Field Champion of Record is determined by the Board of Directors of the American Kennel Club. The present system, adopted in 1946, requires a total of 120 points, which must include three first places at Member or Licensed Field Trials.

There are two types of Sanctioned Field Trials—A and B. Plan A is designed to qualify new clubs for holding licensed

Sire and Son—Both Great Producers of Field Champions

At left above, Fld. Ch. Skeds Captain, sire of 43 field champions including seven in one litter of eight from Fld. Ch. Scrubgrass Sue. At right above, his son, Fld. Ch. Captain of Glenwood, sire of 36 field champions. Both hounds were named "All American" in 1947 by *Sports Afield*. Photos, courtesy of Russell Bennett.

trials. It is a two-day trial, and held in accordance with all rules except that no championship points are awarded. Plan B is less formal, requires no premium list, and may be for one day or more. To apply for a licensed trial, a club must have successfully accomplished two Plan A trials, held at least six months apart, and with at least 40 hounds entered and run.

The "Spring Derby" Trials originated in 1921 by Mr. Osborne Jenkins of New Philadelphia, Ohio, have blossomed into tremendous popularity. In order to compete in these trials, a Beagle must be within the derby age group. A Beagle remains a derby through the second December 31 following its date of whelping. After that time, the dog is no longer eligible for entry in the Spring Derby Trials. In no small way, the Spring Derby Trials were partly responsible for an accelerated breeding program, a keener interest in Beagling, and the ascendancy of the Beagle to top dog in A.K.C. registrations in 1953, a spot which it held for a few years. Credit for the tremendous growth of Beagling and field trials must also be given to *Hounds and Hunting,* the Beagler's magazine, and its editor, I. W. ("Ike") Carrel, who has done so much for the sport as a breeder, competitor, handler, and judge, and through his untiring literary efforts during the past thirty-four years.

The average Beagle club owns or leases its running grounds and keeps it stocked with rabbits. In those States where importation of rabbits for stocking is prohibited, clubs use other means to assure a plentiful supply of game, such as making brush piles and planting feed and cover crops. Clubs situated where the winters are rough have a number of "feeding stations" located throughout the grounds. Through the winter when there is little natural food for the rabbits, club members keep these stations filled with pellets, alfalfa, lettuce, apples, or other suitable feed. Kennels are usually located on the grounds, and there the Hounds can be securely housed during the day or for the duration of the trial. Most clubs also have a clubhouse on the grounds, some very modest, some quite elaborate, all serving the same useful purpose.

Picture taken in 1942 of I. W. (Ike) Carrel, editor of *Hounds and Hunting*, with some of his well-known hounds, whose names are found in many pedigrees.

Field Trial clubs usually close entries and start the drawing at 8 or 8:30 a.m. No entries are accepted after the entries close. It is wise to arrive at the field trial headquarters well in advance of the advertised starting time, especially so if it is necessary to drive some distance from home. By arriving early, the Hound will have more time to get over the ride and get his "feet on the ground" again.

The Beagler first fills out an entry blank which is available at the secretary's table. Specific information must be listed in the spaces provided, namely, the class in which the Hound will compete; dog's name; color; sex; date whelped; registration number or litter registration number; sire and dam; owner's name and address; and name of handler.

The measuring committee then measures the Hound to be certain that it is entered in the proper class. Classes at Licensed Trials are divided by size and sex; at sanctioned trials, usually by size only. The measuring gauge is placed loosely across the shoulder blades at the highest point, the Hound standing in a natural position with his feet well under him. Hounds measuring 13 inches or less are eligible for the 13 inch class only; those measuring over 13 inches but not over 15 inches are in the 15 inch class. Hounds measuring over 15 inches are disqualified from running at Beagle field trials.

After all Hounds are entered and measured, the drawing takes place. The secretary has recorded in his notebook the names of the entries and each is given a number. For the drawing, the more progressive clubs employ a "bingo cage" such as those used in bingo games. Many clubs still use the drawing card system. The Beagle whose number corresponds to the first number selected is the first Hound in the first brace; second number, second Hound in the first brace; third number selected is the first Hound in the second brace; fourth number, second Hound in second brace, and so on until all numbers are drawn. Some clubs list the braces on a large blackboard, making it easier for the judges, handlers, and spectators to copy the order of the running. The running of the Hounds as so drawn is known as the "first series." Should there be an odd number of entries, the last one drawn is known as the "bye" Hound and his brace-mate will be selected by the judges from amongst the other entries after all have run. The bye Hound's bracemate most often is one that showed some qualifications but had considerable interference from his bracemate, preventing him from showing to advantage, thus deserving another opportunity to run a rabbit.

Up to the present time, cottontail trials have been run in braces. Due to the number of entries at many of the modern day trials and the limited time in which to run off a class, some Beaglers are advocating the discontinuance of braces and the substitution of small packs of three to five Hounds.

The drawing completed, the trial is now in charge of the Marshal who has been appointed by the field trial committee which is the managing body for the trial. The Marshal should be selected for his knowledge of the running grounds, his capacity to interpret the rules, his understanding of procedure, and his ability to coordinate his co-workers efficiently for conducting a smooth-running trial. Very often the field trial committee chairman will serve as Marshal. The Marshal usually has two assistants, one to keep the gallery under control at a respectable distance from the running Hounds in order to preclude their interfering with the race, the other to act as a liaison between the Marshal, gallery, and headquarters. The Marshal has selected a group of "beaters" or "brushers" who spread out and move forward at his direction in an orderly fashion until a rabbit is jumped, at which time we hear that excited shout, "Tally-ho!" the universal exclamation for the occasion. After the tally-ho, all brushers group together and remain so until the brace has completed its run. At the conclusion of the run, the Marshal blows his hunting horn or a whistle and the next brace is called. Handlers must keep themselves informed of the order of the running and be ready within hailing distance when their Hounds are called by the Marshal when so directed by the judges. Any Hound absent more than fifteen minutes when thus called is disbarred. The next brace proceeds from a point selected by the Marshal. An efficient Marshal covers the ground methodically and strives to run each brace on ground not used by the previous brace.

Classes at cottontail field trials are judged by two judges. One of the major problems in recent years has been the developing of the number of capable judges necessary to keep pace with the increasing number of trials. There are many qualifications in the make-up of a field trial judge. He must have well-balanced judgment; be honest above reproach; fair to all contestants; physically fit to follow Hounds on foot or mounted, day after day; familiar with the A.K.C. running rules, with the capacity to interpret them intelligently. Last but by no means least, he must have a thorough knowledge of Hound work. This knowledge is attained by years in the field following Beagles, good, bad, and indifferent, watching their moves and actions and being able to evaluate both the meritorious and faulty methods of handling a rabbit.

When ready to start the class, the first brace is called, the two judges look over the Hounds to ascertain their identity, the two Hounds are cut loose, and the Marshal, brushers, judges, and the two handlers follow along in the prearranged direction.

Handling of the Hounds plays a very important part in the training of field trial Hounds. A Hound that handles well will hunt within reasonable range of his handler, obey commands for changes in direction, and come when called. This type of Hound is a pleasure to handle and is easily picked up when a tally-ho is called. The Hound that skirts off in the wrong direction or disappears entirely and pays little or no attention when called is a time waster, surely most embarrassing to the handler, especially when there is a tally-ho and several minutes are lost in locating and catching the Hound. Invariably when this happens, someone will shout, "Hurry up with that Hound; the line is getting cold." True, the line is getting cold, and the more time lost, the less chance the brace has to get off to an auspicious start.

If one of the Hounds in a brace starts his own rabbit, the

bracemate is harked in and both are under judgment. If a tally-ho is called, both handlers catch their Hounds and bring them to the point of the tally-ho, where the judges order them put on the line and the race is on. When Hounds have been laid on a line together or have harked in to one another, the duties of the handlers cease until further instructed by the judges. If a brace becomes split, the Hounds going away on different rabbits, they are ordered up and a new start is made on new game.

Experienced judges usually hold fast until they are sure that the Hounds are getting away on the line. This is to prevent interference with the Hounds should they "run out of track" after covering a very short distance, an incident which happens frequently. In such cases, by immediately rushing after the Hounds, there may be just enough interference to prevent the brace from eventually getting themselves straight, and off to a good run. When the Hounds are away, the judges and handlers follow, but at all times the handlers should stay behind the judges.

Mounted judges have an advantage over foot judges in that they are that much higher off the ground and can view the work of the Hounds from a greater distance. It is unfortunate that the terrain in many parts of the country is not suited for mounting the judges. When on foot, the judges necessarily follow closer to the Hounds to observe the work. Inexperienced judges and handlers will many times run up too close on the Hounds in their earnest desire to catch every bit of the work, thus hindering the efforts of the brace in untangling a check. "Check" is the Beagler's term for a temporary loss. Well-experienced judges seldom get into this situation. The exception is usually caused when the rabbit doubles back on its own line. This is called a "double" and is perhaps the most difficult of all checks for a Hound to pick, certainly even more so if the judges and handlers have trampled on the line. The cottontail leaves one of the faintest scents, possibly the faintest of any game animal pursued by Hounds, and it is indeed a credit to the scenting ability of the Beagle that he can follow the intricate trail of this little bundle of fur.

96

These handlers have just dropped their Hounds on a line which went out through the birches. Judges are standing back out of the picture in a position where they can view the Hounds without crowding them.

Judges Bob Hunt and Art Curren scoring a brace after their run.

One of the A.K.C. rules under which the trials are conducted just about sums up the way the Hounds should run. The rule: "Undue credit shall not be given for speed and flashy driving if the trail is not clearly followed. Accuracy in trailing, voice, endurance, starting ability, style and obedience shall be the principal points of merit, but nothing in the foregoing shall excuse a Hound for pottering, swinging, skirting, babbling, leaving checks, racing, running in a hit-or-miss style, backtracking, running mute, running a ghost trail, all of which shall be considered demerits."

Another important rule reads in part:—"At a check, they should work industriously, close to where the loss occurred, before going further afield to look for the line."

Experienced Beagle men and judges should be capable of analyzing the work of the Hounds in relation to the foregoing rules.

There are far too many rules to detail here. The A.K.C. booklet, "Beagle Field Trial Rules and Standard Procedures" is available from the American Kennel Club, 51 Madison Ave., New York, N.Y. 10010, and is free if ordered singly. All field trialers should have a copy to better understand the rules under which they compete.

Glenn Black, nationally known authority on Beagling and author of *American Beagling,* describes the perfect Hound as follows: (1) runs all of his line; (2) picks checks, if any, promptly; (3) tongues always and only when making headway on a true line; (4) goes like hell.

Some Hounds will "whip" or "weave" a line; that is, they will run to one side of the line, cross it, run the other side, and so on, continually doing this on a straight running rabbit. Some Hounds run so far off the line as to create a loss. Some never recover, while others eventually work back to the original line and continue. However, all of the above constitute faulty action and Hounds performing so rarely advance beyond the first series.

The manner in which a Hound picks a check is perhaps the most decisive factor in his winning a place, provided other work is on a par with the better Hounds in the class. If the rabbit makes a sharp turn, the driving Hound will

Zeke Bonura, former Chicago White Sox home run king with his recent Field Champion, Cane Brake Tony.

This picture, taken in 1948, shows Johnny Vander Meer, famous Cincinnati Reds pitcher of no-hit fame, with his wife and daughter, and Mr. Henry J. Colombo. The string of Shady Shores Beagles are (l. to r.) Snapback, Snapper, Saintly, Skimmer, Sweet Pea, Skylark, Stylist, Sepia, Swishy, and Sportsman.

99

usually overrun. The faster the drive, the further they are likely to overrun. The level-headed Hound, discovering he is out of scent, will put on the brakes and get back as quickly as possible to the point where he actually overran. Using this point as a hub, he should do either of two things: (1) work out a short distance in one direction, then another and another until he hits the line, or (2) cast in a small circle and, if the line is not picked up, gradually widen the circle until he does so. The quicker and closer to the point of the loss that a Hound picks the check, the more credit he receives. Of course he must not give tongue while working a check (this is called babbling), only doing so the instant he strikes the line and takes it away. The judges must decide if a loss is an actual check, or one created by the Hounds themselves through faulty running. In the latter case, no credit should be given. For example, a brace running a straight running rabbit in cover that presents no hazards such as burnt ground, sand, ledge, or water, should not come to a loss, work the check for a minute or more and then continue on in the same straight line. If they had stuck to the true line there would have been no check. When Hounds stop driving for a few seconds and then continue on, there are many of us who define this as a short pause in the run and do not term it a check.

The term "swinging Hound" is given to one which, upon coming to a check, races in a wide circle in hit-or-miss fashion and may hit the line fifty or more feet away from the check. This type of Hound cannot be given much consideration.

The "pottering" Hound, at a check, will cover the ground very slowly, sticking very close to the point where he ran out of scent, very often going over the same piece of ground again and again. While the potterer, if given enough time, may pick the check, in many cases he "dies" right there. This is called close Hound work by many, but it avails nothing if the run ends in a loss at this point. There are some who say they prefer a Hound to stick close to his check and lose his rabbit, to the one that "swings out a mile" and hits the line. However, neither of the two get anywhere at a field

100

FIELD CHAMPION MILL RUN MICKEY (left) and FIELD CHAM-
PION MICK'S MERT, littermates.

Maurice Samson, owner of Watatic
Kennels, posing Field Ch. Watatic Jill

Helen Samson posing Field Ch. Watatic Debbie

Homer Larmay, Kingsford, Michigan, posing his Field Ch. Trigger XVIII

FIELD CHAMPION CONTENTNEA JACK II

trial in comparison to the Hound that picks the checks fast and clean.

Theoretically, a Hound should tongue (give voice) on every bit of the line he is running, keeping his mouth shut when working a check or at any time he has no scent. The Hound that tongues in several directions when dropping on a line, when working a check, or during other parts of the run when he has no scent, is considered "mouthy" or "loose tongued" and gets little consideration.

Some rabbits, when suddenly kicked out of their squat, become frightened. It is the belief of many, including myself, that such a rabbit leaves little or no scent for as much as fifty feet. I have seen Hounds dropped on this type of line "make game" and work the line, sometimes with help from the handlers, to a point where there is scent, giving no tongue to this point, then put on a high class performance. Experienced judges can sense this situation and do not demerit the Hounds for not tonguing those first twenty-five to fifty feet of the line.

The Hound that leaves "gaps in the line" opens only here and there while running the true line. This Hound is considered tight mouthed, makes a poor bracemate, and has little chance to place.

Aside from quitting cold, perhaps the two faults considered most undesirable in a Beagle are running mute and backtracking. The mute Hound runs the line silently, giving no tongue, while the backtracker runs a line to a certain point, reverses himself and runs the same line back to the starting point, or at least for a considerable distance, usually tonguing both ways. A field trial is not the place for these Hounds. In fact, no Beagler should keep such Hounds once it is definitely established that they have these faults.

Running a "ghost trail" has not been common in my experience. This term is applied to the occasion when a Hound runs an imaginary line for quite some distance in the same manner as if on a true line.

At the conclusion of each heat, the term applied to each run by a brace, the judges makes a few notations in their notebooks as to the good or bad features of the run by each

103

of the Hounds and gives each Hound a percentage score. The judges usually agree on which is the better of the two Hounds before they are ordered up. Although there is a general fundamental method of judging, there is no set standard wherein all judges see eye to eye and award the same score to any particular Hound. This is left to the judges involved at each individual trial, and, happily, it works out in most cases to the satisfaction of the majority.

At the conclusion of the first series, the judges decide which Hounds they deem worthy of bringing back into the second series. Be it six, eight, ten, or more, they are brought back in the order of their percentage points. The Hound with the highest score is the first Hound in the first brace and so on in order down the line. However, should two Hounds that were braced together in the first series have scores that would bring them together again (a rarity in these days of large classes), the one with the lower score exchanges places with the Hound with the highest score in the next succeeding brace. The rules state that no two Hounds can be braced together in more than one series.

At the completion of the second series, the judges review the running to this point and list the Hounds in the order of their standing. The winners, first, second, third, fourth, and reserve, may be announced at this time, *provided that all placed Hounds have beaten the Hound placed directly beneath them in direct competition.* However, if this be not the case, additional series are run until this proviso has been fulfilled.

All place Hounds must compete in the second series, a situation that was not always so. At one time, judges could, and did occasionally in small classes, hold out the top dog in the first series and bring back his defeated bracemate as the high Hound in the second series. If this Hound successfully defeated his position, the Hound held out became the winner of first place on the strength of his first series run, hardly fair when you consider that the other place Hounds ran two or more times to earn their places. As Beagling progressed, outmoded practices such as this one were corrected by improving the rules.

Down through the centuries, the Beagle was considered primarily a pack Hound, and today there are Beaglers who feel some form of pack running should be included in cottontail field trials. As of this writing, a few clubs are planning experimental trials at which all of the second series Hounds will be run together as a pack. The proponents of this plan are of the opinion that to become worthy of the "Field Champion" title, a Hound should prove he has the stamina to hold up for about two hours in a pack run, and also that he will not "blow up" under the strain of pack running where competitive pressure is much greater than with only one bracemate. Furthermore, all the Hounds will be down at the same time on the same rabbit under the same conditions, giving each Hound an equal opportunity. It remains to be seen if this plan is practical. Such a drastic change in procedure, even though it proves satisfactory, may not find smooth sailing for nation-wide acceptance.

We have not attempted here to go into every fine detail of cottontail field trialing, but rather have covered the sport in a general way. To the initiated, I need not extol the many virtues of the field trial sport. To the prospective Beagler, I heartily recommend that you join a Beagle club and attend the trials with your Hound. You will love the friendly competition, win or lose; you will enjoy the benefits of a healthy outdoor sport; the association with other Beaglers will bring you many new friends; you will derive considerable satisfaction and pride in training and developing a winner; and last but not least, surely you will find a new interest in life, for the merry little Beagle has done so much for so many.

The Hall of Fame

Fld. Ch. Payne's Marsha, 1957

In 1957 the magazine *Hounds and Hunting* initiated a "Hall of Fame" to honor great Beagles of the past.

On this and the pages that follow, many of the hounds thus honored are pictured, together with note of the year in which they were named.

The publishers are indebted to I. W. Carrel, Robert F. Slike, and Carl Grover for the pictures.

Fld. Ch. Yellow Creek Sport, 1957

Fld. Ch. Gray's Linesman, 1957

The Hall of Fame

Fld. Ch. Grover's Nesco
Forger, 1958

Int. Fld. Ch. Pleasant Run
Diplomat, 1959

Fld. Ch. Sammy R, 1960

The Hall of Fame

Fld. Ch. Nu-Ra Buddy, 1959

Alibi Billy, 1961

Fld. Ch. Sheik of Shady
Shores, 1961

Fld. Ch. Afton's Uncle Sam, 1962

Fld. Ch. Shady Shores Select, 1962

The Hall of Fame

Fld. Ch. Pageline Parson,
1963

Fld. Ch. Wilcliffe Boogie,
1964

Fld. Ch. Bill Ben Sugar,
1957

Fld. Ch. Elrich's Yellow Creek Nifty,
1960

The Hall of Fame

Fld. Ch. Pleasant Run Banker
1963

Fld. Ch. Car-E-Line Buddy
1965

Fld. Ch. Ch. Nottaway Wink
1965

The Hall of Fame

Int. Fld. Ch. Wilcliffe Bannister
1966

Fld. Ch. Dickie's Argo Al
1968

Fld. Ch. Pleasant Run Postman
1966

The Hall of Fame

Fld. Ch. Pearson Creek Countess
1969

Fld. Ch. Hunsicker's Rob Roy
1968

Judging Field Trials

By Lew Madden

ANY one interested in becoming a field trial judge should, if possible, attend one of the judging schools sponsored by the American Kennel Club where qualified instructors will teach you all the fundamentals of your intended career. Experience, observation, and willingness to learn and accept advice will then polish your skills in proportion to your aptitude. Humility for being chosen to rule on entries of fellow Beaglers who are just as well—and in many cases better, qualified to judge hound qualities than you—a courteous explanation of points of issue, and the ability to work and cooperate with your fellow judge are assets that will insure you plenty of assignments. Remember this, however wise you might consider yourself, you are working for experts. If you cannot attend one of the judging schools or if you plan only to participate rather than judge, perhaps a few suggestions will help.

The best way I can present these suggestions is to explain how I try to look at hounds when judging. The first thing a hound *must* do is run his rabbit. How he runs it is not important at this time. That he *can* run it and keep running it is the prime factor. He must accomplish something so that you can evaluate his performance. This you do as he runs his chase. Remembering that the only link the hound has with his quarry is the scent of the trail, and the closer he stays to that trail the better, his best chance of gaining your approval is to maintain constant contact with it. His next step is to make progress along the trail. This progress should be made as rapidly as possible or as slowly as necessary. He should follow the trail just as fast as he can and still keep complete control of it. Otherwise he is not putting forth his best effort to overtake his quarry. When rapid progress accurately is impossible, he should slow his pace as needed to hold contact with the trail. He should indicate all progress by giving tongue and remain silent when not moving forward along the line. When he loses contact with the trail, he should remember where he last had it and work in a sensible manner from that point. He should work independently of his bracemate at all points of loss, yet cooperate with him by immediately claiming a find and hark quickly when his bracemate signals a find. He should be competitive in trying to beat his bracemate but not to the point of jealousy that would interfere with the steady progress of the chase. Beating his bracemate means doing the majority of the work necessary to keep the chase in progress. The hound that passes his bracemate on a straight line proves only that he is faster. If he cannot recover the trail at the next point of loss there is no advantage in getting there first and he looks bad when the hound behind him makes the recovery. Despite this, I prefer the hound that runs in front, if he has the brains and nose to go with his speed. The first hound to arrive at a check has the first chance of solving it. If he is experienced and has good control of himself, that split-second advantage is sometimes all he needs to recover the line before his bracemate has a chance to size up the situation. Speed is an advantage only when controlled, a decided disadvantage when *not* properly controlled, and probably causes more interruptions in the chase than all other reasons combined. Almost any hound is able to run faster than he is capable of trailing his game. Good hounds realize this and pace themselves according to their ability to follow the scent.

Diligence, concentration, accuracy, honesty, independence,

114

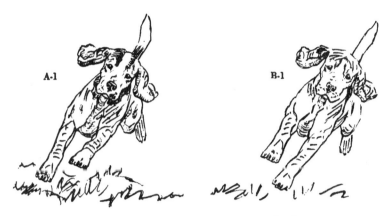

A-1   B-1

Beagle turning left handed while running hard

A-1 is a good mover. He is on the proper lead i.e., he is landing on his
right fore foot. The left will be the second to hit the ground. B-1 is a poor
mover. He will not have the balance or finesse of movement that A-1 will
have. B-1 is in the same phase of stride but he is landing on the left fore
foot.

A-2   B-2

A-2 shows the good mover on his left fore foot which is more under his
center of balance. B-2 being on wrong lead does not have the support
under his center of balance for the turn.

A good dog like a good horse *must* move on the proper lead.

Sketch by Paul Brown, courtesy Gaines Dog Research Center

115

cooperation and competitive spirit are all assets to a good field trial hound and conducive to a good rabbit chase. A hound should be diligent at all times when afield. He should work diligently to locate game and, once routed, to pursue it relentlessly in an effort to overtake it. He should concentrate on adhering to the line, not to show you where the rabbit has been but as the surest method of keeping track of, and advancing toward, his quarry. Hounds that follow a trail merely because they like to puzzle it out and show no desire or intention of overtaking the quarry are not serving the purpose for which the breed was created.

Accuracy is the ability to keep control of the line consistently, to realize loss of scent immediately, to proclaim all progress and to remain silent except when making progress along the line. The hound that tongues when he does not have scent is a liar; the one that does not tongue when he has it and can make progress is a thief. The hound that smells the line and stands around in one spot giving tongue, although he is unable to move it, or tongues the same line over and over, is an imbecile. He keeps saying, "Here it is, here it is," when what we want him to say is, "Here it goes." He is contributing nothing and is probably interfering with his bracemate's chances of moving the line forward.

Independence is a wonderful characteristic in a hound. It enables him to concentrate on his job of running his rabbit and rely on his own abilities. He is not easily influenced by the actions of his bracemate or repeatedly fooled by dishonest hounds. Cooperation is the ability in a hound which enables him to work harmoniously with other hounds. At a loss he will proclaim his find immediately and honestly, giving his bracemate a chance to get in quickly and move forward with him. He will work quietly and independently at his checks, not interfering with his bracemate in any way and, if the bracemate finds first, will hark in at once to help move the line on to the next check. He seems naturally to have the attitude that two hounds can run a rabbit better than one, and if his bracemate is of a similar kind, he is so right.

Competitive spirit is an asset only to a degree. Beyond that

116

certain degree it is a liability. As long as a hound remains accurate in his work and concentrates on running his rabbit it is good for him to have the desire to do it quicker and faster than his bracemate. In field trial competition he is required to defeat the other hound and it is good to have him want to do just that, but beyond a certain point this spirit becomes the main reason for the downfall of many an otherwise good hound. Once a hound decides to beat his bracemate at all costs and concentrates on doing it at the expense of good workmanship, he is very likely to take not only himself but his bracemate as well out of the field trial. You will often hear the expression, "I beat him from behind." Actually no hound ever beats another from behind. He might win from behind but this is because the hound in front is beating himself by not properly doing his work, possibly from an overly competitive spirit. The hound in the rear wins because he concentrates on his work and takes advantage of the front hound's mistakes.

The foregoing gives you a fairly good picture of the qualities which you should look for in your hounds and which a judge will credit to the performers. Now it is time to look into the faults you are likely to see and which call for demerit. Many people confuse faults with mistakes but there is a difference. In my book a fault is one of two things. It is either a bad habit, developed by repeating the same mistake over and over without realizing it, or an inherited characteristic. In other words, faults can be either inherited or acquired. When a hound displays a serious fault repeatedly he has lost his value as a field trial performer. Mistakes are not nearly as serious. A mistake can be corrected and overcome. A judge with little use for a faulty performer is unlikely to criticize severely honest mistakes made in the heat of competition or under unusual circumstances, especially if the performer realizes his error and tries to rectify it.

Quitting is the worst fault a hound can have. It is unforgivable. Once a hound quits, his performance is over. He cannot be judged if he does not perform. Backtracking, if performed as a fault with no realization by the hound of what he is doing, would likely run a close second. It serves

117

no useful purpose and removes the hound farther from his goal of overtaking his quarry. However, if a hound in the heat of battle suddenly grabs a backtrack, or if he harks in and goes a short distance with another that is on a back line, judges are not likely to penalize such performance too severely if the hound recognizes his mistake and corrects it. Under certain circumstances judges may give the hound credit for his intelligence.

Backtracking and quitting are two faults that end the chase. There is no further forward progress when these faults are committed.

Next, we will discuss the faults which slow down the chase: pottering and anchoring. The pottering hound never seems to get anything done. He can do a lot of work on a small amount of rabbit track. He does not seem to know, or if he does know he doesn't seem to care, that there is a rabbit on the front end of the track and that he should be getting closer to it. Trailing conditions seem to have no meaning for him. He makes it look just as hard on a good trailing day as when conditions are poor. He seems more intent on puzzling out every footprint and explaining it than in moving his game. He dramatizes everything he does and fools a lot of people into thinking he is performing under difficult conditions. Oddly enough, many hounds with this fault are capable of running a good rabbit. Quite often they will start out making steady progress and continue it for quite some distance, then for some unknown reason, start pottering along. Once started on this useless motion they never seem to get back to moving their game steadily again. They seem content to follow it at a slow pace with no thought of gaining ground. A good hound will slow down when necessary but he is always working toward the moment when he can progress his line more rapidly and will do so at the first opportunity. The potterer has no such thought in mind.

Anchoring is the fault of running a rabbit up to a point, and then being unable to figure where it went, dwelling right there where he had traced the last footprint. Generally these are close-working hounds and working close is conceded to be a good trait, but there is a limit even to good traits. A hound should work close to his last point of contact with the trail for a reasonable length of time, but after he has explored every possibility in the vicinity of his loss without success he should explore further afield to try to make contact. Not so the anchorer. He will dwell right there and, as some Beaglers describe it, "die beautifully on the line." The anchoring hound, in my opinion, lacks brains and intelligence. He never seems to realize that not being there, the trail must be somewhere else and that if he wants to recover it he must leave that spot. Usually he will return to and tongue on the last inch of scent time after time, often calling back a good bracemate that had intelligently moved out to recover the line in order to perpetuate the chase. Many readers have seen or worked with men who worked hard all day but got little or nothing done. They were always busy but accomplished nothing. The pottering hounds and anchoring hounds are like these men.

Next come the hounds that interfere with, or upset the balance, of the chase. These are the speeders, the over-competitive hounds, the skirters, the liars and the cheats. They often cause a good bracemate to make a bad showing. The excessively fast hound usually carries his bracemate beyond the turns in the trail, causing him to overrun much farther than he ordinarily would. It is hard for a hound to resist following another that apparently has a hot line right between his legs and is making time with it. The over-competitive hound often takes in a lot of territory and frequently hits the line somewhere out ahead, not permitting his bracemate to carry through consistently. His overly competitive spirit causes him to attach more importance to beating his bracemate than to following his quarry and so he becomes erratic in his work. The skirter cuts out around his properly running bracemate, using him as an anchor, in an attempt to intercept the trail ahead or sometimes to avoid some of the hard work. The liar keeps calling his bracemates to points where there is no line and causes them to lose time which he could put to better use by looking in places of his own selection. The cheat has the line but does not claim it properly, thereby denying his bracemate a chance to get in and help move the

119

trail forward. Hounds of this sort are disconcerting to a good, competing hound as he never knows where they will turn up next. So are the over-competitive hound and the skirter. To run with any of these types a good hound must be calm and independent if he is to make a good showing. He deserves an almost unlimited amount of credit if he is able to do so.

You are likely to see the above faults at any field trial. An over-competitive hound may be extremely or mildly over-competitive. The mouthy hound may be excessively mouthy or given to a few extra barks. He may interfere with the progress of the chase to a great degree or hardly at all. You will demerit him according to the degree and number of offenses he commits and credit him for his good accomplishments. Then you will compare his overall performance against that of the other contestants in the class, thereby determining whether or not he is worthy of further consideration. If so, you then determine his relative position among the other contestants still under consideration. With this accomplishment you have just completed your first series judging. Your second series will be composed of the hounds that performed best in first series. The hound that you scored highest will be the first hound in the first brace. The hound with the next best score will be his bracemate and so on down the line, bringing each hound back in the position his score indicates. However, no two hounds shall be braced together in more than one series. Every hound brought back into second series is to be considered as having a chance to win, except that no hound can place above any place hound by which it has been defeated in a previous series. When you are finished, each place hound must have defeated, in direct competition, the hound placed immediately below it and must have been defeated in direct competition by the hound placed inmediately above it.

Having discussed hound faults at length, now we will deal with some of the virtues we desire in our hounds. Nothing is more desirable in an otherwise good hound than a good voice. The louder the better. A good, strong, positive voice on a hound makes you sit up and take notice. It also makes other hounds take notice. Nothing is more thrilling to hear than a good-voiced hound proclaiming his finds and advertising his progress in a positive manner. There are three generally acknowledged types of hound voices: chop, bawl, and squall, and variations of them described as fast chop, short bawl, and short bawl and chop, etc. Some hounds are also called bugle-mouthed and turkey-mouthed. Probably the least desirable mouthed-hound is the squealer. As a hound owner, you should insist on good voices in your hounds.

It is up to the breeder to put volume and quality of tone in his hounds' voices. As a judge, you will be concerned only with how the hound uses his mouth. He should claim quickly on finding the line and steadily to denote all progress, but shut up immediately when he loses it and remain silent until he recovers. If he does this he is a perfect-tonguing hound regardless of type and volume of voice. In competition this serves several purposes. His tongue gives credit for all of his accomplishments and it notifies his bracemate or packmates that the trail has been recovered and the chase is once again in progress. His silence gives the other hounds an opportunity to work on their own initiative, unhampered by false alarms. Hounds, smart hounds especially, soon learn to trust or distrust their running mates and will hark quickly to those they trust. If fooled once or twice by a faulty tonguer, they may lose confidence in him and sometimes fail to honor him even when he is right. I do not criticize such hounds severely for not getting in as quickly as desirable, especially after I have learned to mistrust the faulty tonguer myself. It takes self-confidence to ignore the call of another hound claiming game but only a stupid hound, or person for that matter, is fooled by the same thing time after time.

One of the greatest qualities in a field trial hound is his determination to stay where he belongs and work properly. Most chases come to an end because hounds are not working properly where they should be. The average field trial hound has enough nose on him to smell the trail if he will stay near it and work. Many times a faulty hound will reach out in an unacceptable manner and hit the line at a distant point, thereby pulling the good hound to him and causing a gap in the run. The good working hound should not be criticized for this gap. If he was where he belonged when he got the call, he had no alternative but to heed it if he wished to stay in the chase, and that is what he is there for in the first place. There would be no advantage for him to lose time following the line through to the place his bracemate had picked it up ahead. It is his duty to get up where the chase is going on and help keep it going.

Since staying where he belongs is considered a good hound quality, let's see what makes a hound do it, which types of hounds are most likely to do it, which are not, and why. Assuming an otherwise good hound, his desire to overtake his quarry would largely influence his rate of speed. His rate of speed with its accompanying momentum would indicate the size of the area he would cover or the distance he would over-run at the checks. The excessively fast hound that cannot con trol his speed during the course of the run spends more time off the trail or getting back to it than he does on it. In contrast, the exceedingly slow hound that follows the trail too meticulously fails to make progress simply because he has no desire to overtake his quarry. The fast or overly-competitive hound is therefore unlikely to be a close worker or at least not close enough to gain approval from an exacting judge. And the extremely slow hound is not likely to get enough accomplished to gain approval.

Beaglers as a whole associate the term "staying where he belongs" with being close, and Beaglers who are radical on closeness think the closer a hound stays the better. From the above, it would seem that the best way to get close workers would be to produce hounds that run slow. The slower they run the less ground they are likely to cover. They will have no desire to overtake their quarry, being satisfied to move along at a rate of progress which assures them a smell of the rabbit's every footprint, explaining it as they go. An extremely slow hound will find a lot of things to explain too, because the rabbit, being followed instead of being pursued, has plenty of time to unfold his bag of tricks for the hound to unravel. A hound of this sort will spend much time performing with minimum accomplishment. This is a useless performance because the hound is showing no inclination to overtake his quarry, the main purpose of a rabbit chase, or any chase for that matter.

The fast and wide-going hound will generally run a lot of rabbit on a good-going day by simply getting after it and denying it a chance to perform any of its many tricks. But if speed happens to be his main asset there will be many days and many rabbits on which he will accomplish much less than even the extremely slow hound. As a judge you will be looking for the hound that can make the most positive progress in the most accurate manner. The hound you seek should be fast when conditions permit, but intelligent enough to slow down to any degree necessary to maintain control of the trail when conditions warrant such actions. He should work as close as necessary and move out as far as necessary and his actions should indicate to you that his every move was calculated to move his game the maximum distance in a minimum of time with no lost motion or gambling. Since no two rabbit chases are ever alike and trailing conditions vary greatly from place to place, it is not possible to establish hard fast rules on closeness, wideness, speed or slowness and say flatly, "This is it. Anything over this is too much. Anything less is not enough." The judge must decide from his observation whether or not the hounds applied the proper methods in the proper proportions in the proper places. This judgment will be based on the success achieved by the performers and the judge's interpretation of the methods used will be governed by his experience and ability to evaluate hound work.

A judge can do many things to equalize the opportunities of the hounds under his jurisdiction. First, he should see that hounds get away properly, and together. Second, he should see that they are not interfered with in any way, while running. Third, if during the course of the heat, some hounds encounter any obstacle such as a roadway, cornfield or gallery that the other contestants do not, and the hounds facing the obstacle are unable to negotiate it after making a proper attempt, he should lift them and give them another rabbit. The judge should always give the hounds the benefit of the doubt at a hole or any other place where he is not certain

123

what happened. Many hounds upon holing, realize that they are done with that rabbit and don't linger too long. If hounds appear to have holed and leave, the judge should look for the hole where they last tongued. That way he is satisfied and if no hole is there he knows surely what they did. Fourth, when hounds are performing in a place where the judge cannot observe them well and they continue to run in such a place, he should lift them and get them out where they can be seen. He can't judge them if he can't see them and there is no value in having them perform under doubtful circumstances. Last but not least, the judge must not be too hasty when picking them up on splits.

The judge should wait until he is sure both hounds are on different game. Often one hound is in error and will hark in to the hound who is right. At other times one hound may not have the courage of his convictions and will leave his line in favor of the stronger willed hound.

A judge should not overlook the good defeated bracemate. That a hound lost his heat does not necessarily mean he is unworthy of further consideration. If he contributed greatly to the chase, especially in running with one of the higher-scored hounds, he may be the second best in the class. It takes a good hound to take a beating without losing composure, and any hound that can and still contribute to the chase, with some good solid licks of his own, should not be overlooked. He is probably much more deserving than others that, although they were brace winners, had things much their own way.

Most of the evaluations the judge must make on the hounds under jurisdiction will be on the checks. Very little of the judging is done on the drives and not too much of the credit given except where hounds are able to keep a steady progress going with a minimum of checks. Some hounds are able to do this, overcoming without hesitation situations that would pose a bigger problem for others. The attitude that the hound just had a good rabbit to run must not be taken. Some hounds simply make their rabbits good.

Since most of the judging is done on the checks, we will discuss them here. Whenever a hound loses contact with the trail and must work to recover it, such a condition is called a check. The intelligence with which he works at his checks and his ability to recover them are the bases on which the judge merits or demerits the hound.

There are three kinds of checks: those made by the rabbit, when it changes course or performs some trick in its effort to elude the hounds; those caused by trailing conditions such as bare spots, wet spots, dry areas, dead spots or change in type of cover or footing, etc.. Then there are checks made by the hounds themselves due to faultiness, instability or just plain dumbness. Whatever the cause, all are checks, and problems to be solved. The method of solution is the judge's basis for evaluating hounds. When a check is made by the rabbit, the judge can assume from the actions of good working hounds and their voices where the check was made If the hounds were progressing rapidly they will probably overrun a short distance from momentum or in hope of getting another smell for going on. As soon as they realize the loss of the line they should hurry back to or near the last point of contact. Different hounds have various successful methods that generally enable them quickly to recover the line near the point of loss. A short tight circle, a quick cast back to the right and left, or several short quick jabs at likely spots are acceptable if they serve their purpose. On these quick recoveries, the hound that makes them gets the credit, but the other hound cannot be criticized if he is working just as closely and intelligently in a different spot. He should be credited for displaying independence instead of following his bracemate. If the check is not recovered immediately, the hounds should then make a well organized search, exploring every likely possibility close at hand. If this fails they should explore farther afield. Their ability to search systematically and intelligently will determine the judge's opinion of them. If they perform satisfactorily, they should not be criticized but given credit if they recover even though they may have left part of the line unaccounted for. In case of a double the judge should not be too harsh on the hound that can overcome it if he doesn't claim too well while working it back to the point where the rabbit left his old trail and took a new course. This is a very difficult and uncertain predicament for a hound to find himself in and he shows his honesty by not claiming when he is not sure. After a rabbit has run a trail in two directions and two hounds have run it one direction it can become very complicated. Hounds that lose rabbits in situations like this, if they work diligently and intelligently and never give up trying, should not be severely criticized for losing their game. Other hounds in similar circumstances that display none of the qualities mentioned above and that are inclined to wander aimlessly and work with less diligence are generally dropped, not because they lost their game but because of their behavior over the loss. The hound that never quits trying and comes up with the long difficult checks should gain the admiration of the judges. Most of them will stick with him as long as necessary for him to make the recovery if he will stay and work properly.

Checks made by trailing conditions may look as if they have been made by erratic hounds on a straight line. Under ordinary trailing conditions hounds should not do this. However, on almost every running grounds you will find a variety of scenting conditions, and as hounds move from one type of cover or terrain to another, they will invariably check to adjust to the new situation. Hounds may occasionally encounter "dead spots" where they are unable to get scent properly. These conditions do not always exist at the same place but seem to change from time to time. It is believed that something in or on the ground under certain atmospheric conditions is the cause. When hounds that otherwise perform well falter in spots like this and perform favorably, one can safely assume that they have encountered an unknown condition; they should be given the benefit of the doubt if they had to leave some of the line unaccounted for. Previous and subsequent performance of the hounds should indicate whether they are of the type that cause their own checks or whether they encounter a mysterious situation.

Hounds that make their own checks are not worth much consideration. They are easily spotted by the experienced hound man, but the amateur might regard them highly. They are always picking checks because they are always making them. They are forever in trouble and are sitting ducks for the wise old hound that is independent enough to ignore them and take advantage of their mistakes. Their problem is usually inability to trail and hold a line that they have right between their legs. They keep jumping away from the line and consequently spend more time off it than on it. They do this when running alone or in competition so it is not caused by an over-competitive spirit. Neither is it caused by lack of nose or poor scenting conditions because the hound's trouble is not smelling the track but staying where he smells it. It is inaccuracy caused by inability to stay put.

The judge's ability to recognize and evaluate to what degree faults were displayed, mistakes were committed or excellency was performed by each contestant and to balance the performance of each contestant against the others is the keynote to his success. Some faults are worse than others, some mistakes are bigger than others and some accomplishments are greater than others. As a final note, if *you* want to be a judge, judge 'em and forget 'em. Try not to remember any past performances because the next time you see the performers they will be starting out with a clean slate. You will find yourself placing hounds that you do not particularly like or would not take home as a gift. You will also find yourself dropping hounds that you would give your right arm to own, but since judging is done on a comparative basis you have to place the ones that get the most done in the best manner on that particular day.

The AKC Standard for Judging Field Trials

5-A. Foreword

(1) The Beagle is a trailing hound whose purpose is to find game, to pursue it in an energetic and decisive manner, and to show a determination to account for it.

(2) All phases of its work should be approached eagerly, with a display of determination that indicates willingness to stay with any problem encountered until successful. Actions should appear deliberate and efficient, rather than haphazard or impulsive.

(3) To perform as desired, the Beagle must be endowed with a keen nose, a sound body, and an intelligent mind, and must have an intense enthusiasm for hunting.

(4) Beagle Field Trials are designed and conducted for the purpose of selecting those hounds that display sound quality and ability to the best advantage.

(5) This Standard of Performance contains descriptions of both desirable and faulty actions. Judges will use it as a guide in evaluating performances, and will credit or demerit hounds to whatever degree their actions indicate quality or fault, and to the extent that these actions contribute to accomplishment, fail to contribute to accomplishment, or interfere with accomplishment.

(6) Judges should approach their work with the attitude that the future welfare of the breed is in their hands, and should make their findings and selections on a basis calculated toward keeping the Beagle useful for both field trials and hunting purposes.

5-B. Definitions—Desirable Qualities

Searching ability is evidenced by an aptitude to recognize promising cover and eagerness to explore it, regardless of hazards or discomfort. Hounds should search independently of each other, in an industrious manner, with sufficient range, yet within control distance of the handler, and should be obedient to his commands.

Pursuing ability is shown by a proficiency for keeping control of the trail while making the best possible progress. Game should be pursued rather than merely followed, and actions should indicate a determined effort to make forward progress in the surest most sensible manner by adjusting speed to correspond to conditions and circumstances. Actions should be positive and controlled, portraying sound judgment and skill. Progress should be proclaimed by tonguing. No hound can be too fast provided the trail is clearly and accurately followed. At a check, hounds should work industriously, first close to where the loss occurred, then gradually and thoroughly extending

128

the search further afield to regain the line.

Accuracy in trailing is the ability to keep consistent control of the trail while making the best possible progress. An accurate trailing hound will show a marked tendency to follow the trail with a minimum of weaving on and off, and will display an aptness to turn with the trail and to determine direction of game travel in a positive manner.

Proper use of voice is proclaiming all finds and denoting all forward progress by giving tongue, yet keeping silent when not in contact with scent that can be progressed. True tongue is honest claiming that running mates can depend on.

Endurance is the ability to compete throughout the duration of the hunt and to go on as long as may be necessary.

Adaptability means being able to adjust quickly to changes in scenting conditions and being able to work harmoniously with a variety of running mates. An adaptable hound will pursue its quarry as fast as conditions permit or as slowly as conditions demand. At a loss, it will first work close, and then, if necessary, move out gradually to recover the line.

Patience is a willingness to stay with any problem encountered as long as there is a possibility of achieving success in a workmanlike manner, rather than taking a chance of making the recovery more quickly through guesswork or gambling. Patience keeps a hound from bounding off and leaving work undone, and causes it to apply itself to the surest and safest methods in difficult situations.

Determination is that quality which causes a hound to succeed against severe odds. A determined hound has a purpose in mind and will overcome, through sheer perseverance, many obstacles that often frustrate less determined running mates. Determination and patience are closely related qualities and are generally found in the same hound. Determination keeps a hound at its work as long as there is a possibility of achievement and quite often long after its body has passed the peak of its endurance. Determination is desire in its most intense form.

Independence is the ability to be self-reliant and to refrain from becoming upset or influenced by the actions of faulty hounds. The proper degree of independence is displayed by the hound that concentrates on running its game with no undue concern for its running mates except to hark to them when they proclaim a find or indicate progress by tonguing. Tailing, or watching other hounds, is indication of lack of sufficient independence. Ignoring other hounds completely and refusing to hark to or move up with running mates is indication of too much independence.

Cooperation is the ability to work harmoniously with other hounds by doing as much of the work as possible in an honest, efficient manner, yet being aware of and honoring the accomplishments of running mates without jealousy or disruption of the chase.

Competitive spirit is the desire to outdo running mates. It is a borderline quality that is an asset only to the hound that is able to keep it under control and to concentrate on running the game rather than on beating other hounds. The overly competitive hound lacks such qualities as adaptability, patience, independence, and cooperation, and in its desire to excell is seldom accurate.

Intelligence is that quality which influences a hound to apply its talents efficiently, in the manner of a skilled craftsman. The intelligent hound learns from experience and seldom wastes time repeating mistakes. Intelligence is indicated by ability to adapt to changes in scenting conditions, to adapt and to control its work with various types of running mates, and to apply sound working principles toward accomplishing the most under a variety of circumstances.

The hound that displays the aforementioned qualities would be considered the Ideal Beagle for all purposes afield, capable of serving as a field trial hound, a gun dog, or a member of a pack, on either rabbit or hare.

Quitting is a serious fault deserving severe penalty and, in its extreme form, elimination. Quitting indicates lack of desire to hunt and succeed. It ranges from refusing to run, to such lesser forms as lack of perseverance, occasional let up of eagerness, and loafing or watching other hounds in difficult situations. Quitting is sometimes due to fatigue. Judges may temper their distaste when a hound becomes fatigued and eases off, if such a hound has been required to perform substantially longer than those with which it is running. During the running of a class a hound may have to face several fresh competitors in succession. In such instances a short rest period would be in order. Otherwise, Judges should expect hounds to be in condition to compete as long as necessary to prove their worthiness, and no hound that becomes unable to go on should place over any immediate running mate that is still able and willing to run.

Backtracking is the fault of following the trail in the wrong direction. If persisted in for any substantial time or distance it deserves elimination. However, hounds in competition sometimes take a backline momentarily, or are led into it by faulty running mates. Under these circumstances Judges should show leniency toward the hound that becomes aware of its mistake and makes a creditable correction. Judges should be very certain before penalizing a hound for backtracking and, if there is any doubt, take sufficient time to prove it to be either right or wrong. Backtracking indicates lack of ability to determine direction of game travel.

Ghost trailing is pretending to have contact with a trail and making progress where no trail exists, by going through all the actions that indicate true trailing. Some hounds are able to do this in a very convincing manner and Judges, if suspicious, should make the hound prove its claim.

Pottering is lack of effort or desire to make forward progress on the trail. Hesitating, listlessness, dawdling, or lack of intent to make progress, are marks of the potterer.

Babbling is excessive or unnecessary tonguing. The babbler often tongues the same trail over and over, or tongues from excitement when casting in attempting to regain the trail at losses.

Swinging is casting out too far and too soon from the last point of contact, without first making an attempt to regain scent near the loss. It is a gambling action, quite often indicating over-competitiveness or an attempt to gain unearned advantage over running mates.

Skirting is purposely leaving the trail in an attempt to gain a lead or avoid hazardous cover or hard work. It is cutting out and around true trailing mates in an attempt to intercept the trail ahead.

Leaving checks is failure to stay in the vicinity of a loss and attempt to work it out, bounding off in hopes of encountering the trail or new game. Leaving checks denotes lack of patience and perseverance.

Running mute is failure to give tongue when making progress on the line.

Tightness of mouth is failure to give sufficient tongue when making progress. This will often be evidenced by the hound tightening up when pressed or when going away from a check.

Racing is attempting to outfoot running mates without regard for the trail. Racing hounds overshoot the turns and generally spend more time off the trail than on it.

Running hit or miss is attempting to make progress without maintaining continuous contact with the trail, or gambling to hit the trail ahead.

Lack of independence is a common fault that is shown by watching other hounds and allowing them to determine the course of action. Any action which indicates undue concern for other hounds, except when harking in, is cause for demerit.

Bounding off is rushing ahead when contact with scent is made, without properly determining direction of game travel.

5-D. Credits

(1) Hounds shall be credited principally for their positive accomplishments. The extent of any credit should be governed by the magnitude of the accomplishment and the manner in which it is achieved. Credit is earned for searching ability, pursuing ability, accuracy in trailing, proper use of voice, endurance, adaptability, patience, determination, proper degree of independence, cooperation, controlled competitive spirit, intelligence displayed when searching or in solving problems encountered along the trail, and success in accounting for game.

(2) When crediting hounds for working style or methods used to gain accomplishments, Judges should keep the purpose of the breed constantly in mind and be alert for hounds, deficient in ability, that make simple problems appear difficult. They also should guard against becoming impressed by fascinating actions that do not produce results. Credit for working style should be used chiefly to differentiate between successful performers, and should never be applied to a degree which might indicate that style or method has been preferred to accomplishment, except in instances where excessive faultiness is involved. Credit for any accomplishment should be in proportion to its contribution to the performance. Mere lack of fault is not grounds for credit. While faultiness is not to be considered lightly, the slightly faulty hound that succeeds should be preferred to the stylist that fails.

5-E. Demerits

(1) Faults, mistakes, lack of accomplishment, and apparent lack of intelligence, shall be considered demerits and shall be penalized to whatever extent they interfere with or fail to contribute to a performance.

(2) Faults are undesirable traits indicating lack of sound quality, and shall be penalized in proportion to the degree of commitment, the frequency of repetition, and the distractions they afford running mates, as well as for the interruptions or lack of progress they cause during the performance. Quitting, backtracking, ghost trailing, and running mute, are the more serious faults. Pottering, swinging, skirting, babbling, leaving checks, racing, running in hit-or-miss fashion, tightness of mouth, and lack of desire or ability to find and move game, shall be considered demerits.

(3) Mistakes are erratic judgments, sometimes committed under pressure of competition and prompted by a desire to excel, and sometimes due to influence of faulty running mates. Where mistakes are not committed with a frequency that would indicate lack of sound quality, consideration should be shown according to the hound's aptitude for realizing its errors, and its efforts to overcome them.

(4) Lack of accomplishment is failure to get enough done to compare favorably with the competition, and is often due to lack of such qualities as determination, patience, intelligence, or endurance. In instances where this is apparent the penalty should be severe. Judgment on hounds that fail to accomplish as desired should be based on the circumstances under which the failure occurred and the determination and intelligence displayed in the effort to overcome it. Where failure is no fault of the hound, such as interference with the game or trail, or where a worthy hound encounters an especially hazardous or abnormal circumstance unlike anything the majority of contestants are expected to overcome, new game should be provided without penalty. Lack of intelligence is apparent in the hound that does not portray sound judgment and skill during its performance.

131

FIELD CHAMPION FLAT SHOALS BUCK

Hare Stakes

BY A. D. HOLCOMBE

THE sport of Beagling has many fascinating aspects and shades of excitement and interest, and one of the most fascinating of all is the pursuit of the snowshoe hare with a pack of fine Hounds. This is primarily a sport of the north country, for the snowshoe hare, or varying hare, as he is sometimes known, ranges across the northern part of North America from one coast to the other. He is found in Canada and in northern parts of the United States from Maine across the northern States to the Pacific Ocean.

Because of his swiftness afoot and his cleverness in laying an excellent, devious trail when pursued, the snow shoe hare has long been the object of the hunter and Beagler, who find him one of the gamest and most elusive of all quarries.

This hare possesses the unusual trait of being able to change color without losing its fur. In winter, after the first snowfall that remains on the ground for longer than a few days, the coat of the snowshoe hare turns from grayish brown to white in one of nature's most effective examples of protective coloration. Hidden against a snow background, a hare is indeed difficult to spot if he chooses to sit tight in his bed, or form, as it is known. Winter also produces other changes in the hare's physical makeup, which are to

133

his advantage. For one thing, his feet grow long hairs between the toes and along their outer edges, forming a sort of snowshoe. When the snows are deep the hare is thus able to skim lightly across the surface, while his enemies, the bobcats, foxes, and Hounds, often founder in the drifts and cannot long pursue him.

In spring, the coat of the hare turns brown once again, and he is thus fitted with protective coloration for his summer existence.

The snowshoe hare appears to be much heavier than his cousin, the cottontail rabbit, but much of this impression is a deception, caused by his build, and his heavy coat of fur, which is his insurance against the severity of northern winters. An extra large hare will weigh from four to perhaps six pounds, whereas an extra large cottontail will weigh about four pounds, or slightly more. The hare has much longer hind legs than the cottontail; they are often nearly as long as his entire body, which lends him a somewhat kangeroo-like appearance. He is long of body, quite slender, and otherwise physically resembles a cottontail rabbit, except that his heavy coat gives him the appearance of being much larger.

The hare prefers to live in or near deep, large swamps, covered with cedars, alders, and evergreens of all kinds— the more brush heaps and ground spruce, the better. On sunny spring or autumn afternoons he may be found sunning himself in some ferns or other light cover along the hillsides that overlook his favorite swamp. In winter he is most likely to be found deep in the swamp, hidden in a network of dark cover. He prefers the so-called Black Growth to all other cover, and whenever the weather is inclement he remains hidden in a dry, sheltered spot most of the time.

Unlike the cottontail rabbit, the hare rarely goes to earth, unless wounded by a hunter, and he is rarely run to a kill by Hounds if he is full grown. A pack of Hounds that is able to run a mature hare to a kill is an excellent pack indeed.

Hunting the snowshoe hare with excellent Hounds is a sport that has no equal in this writer's experience. Those who have never indulged themselves in such a hunt on a crisp autumn or winter day cannot conceive of the kind of enjoyment that awaits them on their first trip. Hare stakes are similarly fascinating, and are conducted on wild game. In either case the procedure is about the same, with the exception that in hunting for the gun one or more hunters set out to make a kill, whereas in hare stakes a pair of judges set out to evaluate the work of a pack of Hounds that are strangers to each other, while the Gallery of Beaglers stands by to observe and listen to the race.

Hunting the snowshoe hare with Hounds has been a popular sport for many years, and in the early 1900's hunters began to hold hare stakes in which to test the relative merits of their Hounds. The first hare stake licensed by the American Kennel Club was held in 1916 by the Northern Hare Beagle Club at North Creek, New York. This club is the oldest known Beagle club to devote its attentions and interest to holding pack stakes on the snowshoe hare. It is still an active organization today, holding one of the finest A.K.C. licensed field trials in the nation annually at North Creek, New York. It is usually held the first week in October, when the full blaze of autumn colors are everywhere spectacularly displayed.

Since 1916 many other hare clubs have come into existence, and today there are some thirty-five of them participating in the sport, all holding pack stakes each year.

The procedure of holding a hare stake is interesting in itself. Early on the morning of a stake, all the Beaglers meet at a prearranged "headquarters," which is usually at the club's grounds, or at a nearby hotel or restaurant if the club does not have a clubhouse of its own, suitable for such a get-together. There they measure in the Hounds, in order to make certain that Hounds under thirteen inches in height are not called upon to compete against the larger class of Hounds, which stand from thirteen to fifteen inches tall at the shoulder. The Hounds, thus measured, are numbered. Each Hound is assigned a number, which is painted on the side of the Hound for identification purposes, in order that the judges can tell one Hound from another swiftly and without making errors of identification during the running. The letters are usually about five inches in height, and in white or yellow colors, depending on the coloring and markings of the individual Hound to be numbered.

The Beagle club sponsoring the stake has previously appointed a field trial committee, which serves during the stakes, carrying out the rules and regulations of the trial throughout. Field Marshals have also been appointed, usually from among the members of the club. It is the function of the Marshals to act as overseers of the trial as it is actively carried out. One Marshal, known as the Gallery Marshal, makes certain that members of the Gallery do not wander about the running grounds after the Hounds have been cast, getting in the path of the hare and turning him unnecessarily or causing a loss, or interfering in any way with the race. He also remains in the Gallery where he watches for Hounds that have quit the race for any reason—for a Hound that pulls out of a race will generally head for the Gallery to seek its master—and the Gallery Marshal warns the handlers of such a Hound that the Hound must be taken back into the race; if he remains out of the running pack for longer than fifteen minutes, the Hound is disqualified from the trial. The Marshal takes the numbers of all Hounds that are thus out of the race, and later hands these to the judges, in order that there will be no mistakes and Hounds that were out of the running for too long a time will not place among the winners.

One Marshal is known as the "judges' Marshal" and it is his job to keep a nearly constant liaison between the judges and the Gallery. His is a running job, nearly as severe as the judges, for he is constantly in touch with the judges, and also in touch with the Gallery. He must know the running area well and be able to give advice to the Gallery as well as to the judges, who may be new to the area. If a split occurs, some Hounds going off on game other than the hare being run, the judges inform their Marshal of this, and he relays the message to the Gallery with the judges' orders— usually either for handlers to pick up all Hounds for a recast, or to get the Hounds in the smaller pack back in with the others. The tasks of the Marshals are vitally important to the success of any hare stake, and the men who handle the job must be well chosen.

The judges themselves are the real key to a successful hare stake, however. They should be able to overcome all obstacles thrown in their way, or dropped there inadvertently by clubs which choose poor Marshals or otherwise do not handle their stake in the best fashion. Judges must be hunters who know well the habits and tricks of the snowshoe hare, from the ways he will attempt to befuddle the Hounds to the most probable course he will run when circling ahead of the pack. They must be familiar and accustomed to running in the woods, know how to get around swiftly and capably, and with a minimum of noise and energy expended. And in addition, they must know the values, positive and negative, of Hound work as it is concerned with pack running.

The procedures involved in running a pack of Hounds on hare, and running a brace of Hounds on cottontails, are as different as day and night, and experience with one will not qualify a man to handle the other properly in any sense of the word. In a hare stake, once game is up and the pack has harkened together and the chase is on, a judge will consider himself fortunate indeed if he is able to see more than one-eighth or one-tenth of the entire race that follows. In a cottontail run, a judge, being on horseback and in fairly open cover most of the time, should be able to see nearly every move two Hounds make.

To the newcomer, judging a hare stake appears to include a great deal of luck, but actually this is not so. It is not necessary for a judge to see one-half or even one-third of the actual work that takes place in a hare race. It is more important that he be able to evaluate what he does see, and that he manage to see the valuable and necessary aspects of the race that can tell him all he needs to know. He must know when to give credit and when to deduct it, and be able to see value in every move of every Hound he sees throughout the day.

The aim of a hare stake is to select from the pack of entries the five Hounds that are the best five, all things considered, in the pack, and rate them in the order of their merit. A Hound should be adjudged winner over his packmates not alone because he was able to lead them all day, nor because he picked one or two or more vital checks; rather he should be selected and set apart with honor *because his overall performance in contributing to the work of the pack was superior to any other individual in the stake.* He should be able to stay up in the front part of the pack all day long, not drag behind most of the time. He should be free of noticeable faults in the style of his work; should work independently of the rest of his packmates, yet harken to those that are not faulty instantly when they announce a "find." He should be able to contribute more than his share of the check work, solving a goodly number of tangles in the trail the hare will surely leave behind. He should not attempt to defeat the pack's work or interests by swinging wide on his casts, stealing the line, or exhibiting other such faults that indicate a Hound is lacking in one or more of the fundamental qualities of trailing and pack work.

Experienced judges are fully aware of the tricks Hounds will attempt in order to win their way over the pack, and will "cut" these Hounds in proportion to the degree that their faulty work impedes the work of the pack. One of the basic methods of judging a pack of Hounds is the device of using the pack as a barometer to test and evaluate the quality of work of the individual Hounds in it. This valuable yardstick is one without which successful and accurate judgment in hare stakes cannot consistently take place. By its application, a judge does not have to see all the work displayed in a stake in order to learn all he needs to know about the competing Hounds.

For instance, when a Hound "ghost trails" (that is, runs an imaginary hare in order to lead the pack, even when there is no hare at all ahead of him), the culprit is soon discerned by the fact that the rest of the pack will not find scent of any hare, and will fail to follow this Hound more than a few yards. Thus the judge knows what has happened when he sees this take place, and he immediately eliminates the errant Hound, once he has made certain the "ghost trailer" is not merely indicating a superior nose. This same principle applies throughout a hare stake, and when Hounds are apprehended while committing serious faults, such as backtracking, line stealing, and so on, they are immediately ordered out of the race, for the work of a pack is repetitious in nature, as is the work of the individual Hound. The finest Hounds do the lion's share of the work, while the faulty and inferior Hounds consistently repeat their faults or poor work. Thus, when a judge finds one of the Hounds under judgment to be inferior to the point of upsetting the smooth running of a pack of Hounds, that Hound is eliminated without delay, for it will only be a matter of time and circumstances until the fault will be repeated.

As one of the greatest of all authorities on hare stakes, Mr. E. C. Hare, Hollidaysburg, Pennsylvania, stressed in his contribution to the work *The Beagle In England And America,* by H. W. Prentice, published in 1920, Beagles "are both imitative and gregarious." In short, they will in time permit their own work to be somewhat influenced if subjected constantly to cheating Hounds in sufficient numbers that they cannot cope with them; also, *that the work of a pack is repetitious.* This latter principle forms the basis of pack running, and judgment thereof, most important to hare stakes, for it is unquestionably true that any given pack of Hounds, once they have worked together long enough to understand each other's work, and have formed a smooth-running pack, will inevitably function much as a machine will function, each Hound carrying out a particular task within the pack consistently as conditions permit him to do so. The amount each Hound contributes to the work of the pack in which he runs is proportional to the conditions present on the day the run takes place, and more importantly, to the individual quality and capability of his packmates. The function of the individual Hound in a pack is thus a relative matter, subject to the quality of his competitors, and once a pack has run together for a few hours, and the faulty Hounds have been eliminated by the judges, the pack will begin working in a consistent pattern, which will be more obvi-

139

ous as time goes on. The length of time required to form a pattern which will be obvious to judges depends on how well the run proceeds, and whether the judge is fast enough and is judging in cover which is clear enough for him to see a great deal of the work during each check. It may be a matter of an hour or so, or it may take all day, and sometimes more time than a trial lasts, though I would say that under average conditions it should not be longer than from two to five hours of running *with faulty Hounds removed* before a pattern which can be perceived by the judges will readily emerge. When once this pattern emerges it will only alter as scenting conditions change, or the Hounds begin to wear down from exhaustion. It is possible to run the same pack of Hounds for five years, and if they do not change individually through their hereditary pattern or physical alterations, they will still continue to perform generally the same integral part and proportion of the work in pack as they performed the day they first ran together, varying conditions considered.

Thus we see that if a hare stake is properly judged, with faulty Hounds being eliminated as soon as possible and the remaining Hounds permitted as much time as they need to begin to work in harmony and to learn each other's capability and traits, and then to participate in accordance with the laws of their natural ability to perform in pack, it becomes relatively simple to judge them, for they will in due time perform in a repetitious manner, and the work of the finest Hounds will thus be the more outstanding and obvious. The more entries in a hare stake, the lesser will be the margin of quality between the top Hounds, and the more time required to judge the Hounds adequately, since more time will be required for them to understand each other, and learn each other's running habits. The final stages of a hare stake will vary widely from the opening phases of the stake.

When a pack of Hounds is first cast, they are likely to do almost anything. They may riot and babble and race against each other and commit almost every error of running style in the book. This is to be expected, since the Hounds have been trained and conditioned to a razor's edge in order to withstand the ordeal of a field trial; also, they have been bred to compete against each other and to perform under the pressure that results from pack running. Consequently, Hounds are not usually judged during the first twenty minutes or so of their race. This gives them time to settle down, and to learn something about the style of the others. Soon they straighten out and get down to the business of running the hare, and most faults will be non-existent, except in those Hounds that are just simply faulty in style, and they are soon weeded out so that the pack will then work "in harness" nicely.

Weeding out the culprits is about the toughest job judges of a hare stake have to perform. Under competition in pack, Hounds with faults indicate them clearly—the problem is to catch them in the act, and this is best accomplished by what is known as getting a "marked line." A judge will know where to station himself in order to catch an occasional glimpse of the hare running ahead of the Hounds. When the hare turns, the judge can well appraise the Hounds under judgment, for when the pack comes streaming through the woods on the trail and the judge knows just what the hare did, he knows which Hounds are following the trail clearly. The Hounds that are leading the pack should be under close scrutiny at marked lines observed by the judge early in any hare stake, for one of the worst culprits is the Hound that wishes to lead the pack at the expense of doing clean, sound work. He is to be found today in nearly every hare stake and should be eliminated as soon as he can be apprehended, for no race can proceed smoothly, except under unusually excellent scenting conditions, as long as such Hounds are permitted to remain in the pack. Such Hounds usually possess excellent noses, and are swift afoot, but are found to be lacking in level-headedness and intelligence. Unable to excel in check work at all, they can "drive" a hare like a demon possessed, and are able to lead the pack because they are not concerned with what happens when the hare turns or twists, or through trickery in his running, attempts to throw off the Hounds from following. When a hare attempts such tactics, these faulty Hounds will shoot far off the end

141

of the trail, usually giving tongue and pulling most of the pack with them. Then, they cast wide hoping to strike the line by luck and perhaps get away from the pack entirely. If they do not strike the line, they must then wait until the pack works out the tough parts, untangles the trail for them, and then these Hounds bounce right back in the lead again. They are the bane of all hare stakes, and should be eliminated as soon as apprehended, and never under any conditions should they be awarded a place among the winners.

The experienced judge knows well the telltale signs of a race that is "broken." This is caused when the race is not smooth and steady, yet the drives are long and fast, indicating that scent is holding well. Most of the time this is caused by the faulty work of certain unknown Hounds in the pack, and then the task of weeding them out begins. Once these few are eliminated, the pack will work harmoniously "in harness," and the race will be smooth and steady. Sensible Hounds know how fast they can drive their hare without overshooting unnecessarily when they reach the end of a straight run, and generally when the culprits are all removed, the pack will not be strung out over many yards, nor will one or two Hounds be leading by more than a few feet for sustained periods.

Once the pack is working in harmony, judgment becomes a simple matter, for the Hounds themselves will tell the judge all he needs to know. This phase of judgment calls for an accurate analysis and interpretation of what he sees, because by now the Hounds have learned those among them that are performing most effectively, and accomplishing most of the work. They reveal this vital information by their actions to those who have the eye to see it. It might be accurately said that the Hounds are judging each other and reflecting their decisions by their own actions.

At this point, the Hounds have used up much of their energy, and stamina has begun to enter on the scene. When a pack is milling about a check area, trying to ferret out which way the hare went, a judge often observes some of the Hounds standing by and watching the work of certain others. These Hounds, quite well tired, are satisfied to stand by and rest for the most part during checks. By now they know from experience which Hounds to watch. By watching these Hounds, they are thus ready to get into pack and go as soon as the line is discovered and the pack is away on the new line. These Hounds are actually pointing to the best Hounds, in effect, and saying, "There are the Hounds that are still carrying most of the load!"

When, toward the end of a trial, a judge sees this happening a few times during the checks, and he watches to see which Hounds actually do pick the checks, he does not have to see a great deal more to know which are the real contenders. It is then just a matter of time until one Hound of the few that are doing most of the work can come to the fore and emerge as the winner. At bit of patience and some careful observation, and the decision is reached readily. *When in doubt, Hounds should always be left to run until all doubt is eliminated—that is a maxim when it comes to judging a hare stake.*

A judge who is careful to spend his time cutting ahead of the pack to get marked lines during the early phases of the race, building up negative work on the Hounds, and eliminating those that impede the pack too much to permit good work, can thus conserve most of his strength for the latter stages of the stake. The work and interpretation of the final hour of a hare stake, to my way of thinking, is worth all the rest of the stake put together, for by now the Hounds that were so eager to split the wind in the early stages are winded and tired, and those that have paced themselves, provided they were in there working and never lagging during the early stages of the run, are now able to assert themselves.

The Hounds that can gain mastery over the pack by dint of sheer courage, will, stamina, and ability, and can take it hour in and hour out, will stand an excellent chance of reproducing this quality—and reproducing better Hounds is at least ninety percent of the value of any kind of field rials or pack stakes.

One of the great Hounds of modern times, able to perform equally well in braccs on cottontail rabbits or in pack on snowshoe hare, is Field Champion Fish Creek Andy, a thirteen incher, in his eleventh year at this writing. It was said of Andy that, "During the first hour of a hare race he didn't show up as being brilliant, but during the second hour he got his packmates out of so much trouble that they followed him during the third hour and thereafter!" Andy would frequently pull out of pack suddenly, and cut off to right angles all by himself in such way as to appear to have left the race. Actually he knew in some uncanny way (probably mostly through his extra-sensitive nose and partly through "patterning" the style of his rabbit) that the hare had turned. Within a matter of seconds the entire pack would harken to him, and sure enough, he had that line right beneath his feet and was going full speed with it. An all day race was no problem to him when in his prime, and he would be all ready to start out the next day and do it all over again. Today, at advanced age, he still gets into pack with the younger, stronger Hounds; despite the fact that his hearing is beginning to fail, Andy shows them an occasional trick or two, but of course he cannot hold up as well as he once did.

Fish Creek Andy is from the Fish Creek strain of Beagles developed over the past forty years by Clarence Jones, Rome, New York. It is doubtful if any better strain of Beagles of overall quality has ever been bred in this country, for they are trained and trialed on both the cottontail rabbit and the snowshoe hare. Thus, they must perform in the flawless style demanded by the cottontail men, yet they must exhibit the fine characteristics such as stamina, and ability to perform under pressure of pack, hour in and hour out, on snowshoe hare.

Many excellent strains of hare Hounds are to be found in this country today, and this limited chapter could not possibly consider them all or properly extend to them the credit they deserve. Some of the finest hare Hounds come from the Watatic Kennels, developed and own by Maurice Samson, Ashburnham, Massachusetts, and there are many other excellent kennels.

The true-blue hare Hound is a top-notch Beagle. He has the

stamina and courage to participate in all-day runs, and the ability to pursue his game hour after hour, long after the swamp, or other cover through which the race may take him, is interlaced with many old tracks of his quarry to make the chase more complex as the race wears on. The real hare Hound must have muscles of steel, a will and nerves of cast iron, and a heart that never knows quit. He must be independent in his style of running, steady in spite of the faults and rioting of inferior packmates, and he must constantly surge forward, pushing the quarry with all the proper speed and capability at his command.

The impression that the best hare Hounds are "wild" in their running style is definitely and completely untrue. Beagles with such personalities will do no more than upset the smooth harmony of an otherwise fine pack, and have no business in a hare race any more than they have in any kind of hunt. In fact, a Beagle that is excitable when running alone or in brace should never be entered in a pack stake, for he will surely react by rioting or babbling or otherwise "upsetting the apple cart."

The true hare Hound must cast wider when searching for game to start, for hare range wide, and a Hound that hunts too close will be at a disadvantage. But, he must be in control while hunted, all the same, and be willing to hunt with the hunter and not go off by himself to search. Then, once game is up and the race is on, he should be in there to the finish as long as there remains a packmate with which to run.

Those who have hunted the great white hare know well the thrills to be encountered in such a hunt. To those who have never hunted this hard going gamester, there are many thrills awaiting you in the northern part of this country. And when you set out to hunt your Hounds on the snowshoe hare, or to trial them in a hare stake in the north woods, make certain you have sound, capable specimens, possessing plenty of stamina and courage, for the white hare is a match for the best of Beagles and will test them long and well.

145

Field Trial Champion Payne's Linda and her owner, Mr. Owen M. Payne. In November 1954, Kentucky Colonel commissions were bestowed upon Mr. and Mrs. Payne in recognition of their contributions down through the years to the breeding and showing of Beagle Hounds in the United States and Canada. So far as can be ascertained, this is the only time that a man and wife were ever jointly commissioned as Kentucky Colonels.

Training the Beagle for Field Work

By Owen M. Payne

SO far as we know, there are no deep dark secrets in the art of field training a Beagle. All that is involved is a measure of common sense, plus a world of patience, understanding, and hard work. No Hound of which we ever heard was trained in the kennel yard or on concrete to run a rabbit, although in a kennel, one can and should begin the preliminary training that is all-important.

Until the puppy has had his anti-distemper and hepatitis shots at the age of about four months, we do not care to enter into any serious efforts at training at all, except to accustom the puppy to sudden sharp and unexpected noises or sounds such as hammering, sawing, the clattering of feed pans, buckets, and so forth, plus the occasional letting off of a small firecracker or the shooting of a blank .22 caliber pistol or rifle cartridge. These latter noises should only be made at feeding time so that the puppy will learn to associate them with a pleasant experience. To a healthy puppy there can be no more pleasant an experience than mealtime.

We should be ever mindful that the more a puppy is handled and made over, the more amenable and tractable he will become as an adult. The less likely he will be to become shy or timid, faults to which too many Beagles are unfortunately prone. Most of this shyness or timidity can be eliminated or prevented by human contact and petting, or "making-over," in the early months of the pup's life. Many shy or timid Beagles have been cured of these most objectionable traits by being placed in the hands of people who have small children, who were permitted and encouraged to play with these shy youngsters to their hearts' content.

After he has had his permanent anti-distemper and hepatitis shots at the age of four months, it is time to begin taking the puppy afield for the first of many, many times. If you are a city dweller, as most Beaglers and Beagle owners are, get yourself a gasoline credit card and a good set of tires for your car. You will need both before you have made a finished performer of your young hopeful. As Rome was not built in a day, neither will you accomplish wonders overnight. Here you will have to learn the meaning of the word patience, for it will probably take all summer to do the job.

It may be said that a Beagle puppy can be trained, or "broken" as we term it, by simply sending him down in the country somewhere, where he will be permitted to run at large with an old Hound of possibly many faults. In time, the puppy will become "broken," or started. This method we by no means advocate. Too likely this self-hunting Hound will become just that—he will hunt when he pleases, where he pleases, and go to the barn to take a nap when he pleases. He will develop, almost surely, headstrong characteristics that will be extremely difficult to overcome, and he is not nearly so apt to become the tractable, lovable hunting companion that you so much desire. Then later, when and if you take him to the field trials, his bull-headedness will be most noxious both to you and to the judges.

The first good many trips afield are not for the purpose of training this young fellow to run rabbits. Rather, they are for the sole purpose of acquainting him with the myriad of things to see, hear, and above all smell, in this hitherto unknown world—to get him "brush wise," so to speak.

If the blackberries are ripe and your wife enjoys picking them, you are a lucky man. You will wind up with some luscious pies and cobblers and your puppy will learn an awful lot without his ever realizing that he is being trained. As he follows along slowly from berry patch to berry patch, his little legs will not become too tired, and he will have ample time to pause here and there to sniff at this bug, that terrapin, and a bit later, at the field mouse.

At first he will not let himself get more than a very few feet away. Later, while the berry bucket is being filled and the puppy's confidence has become a little more established, he will begin to wander a bit further away. Inevitably he will become lost at the great distance of thirty or forty feet, and his cries of distress will be truly alarming. But do not go to the puppy. Let him come to you. Stand perfectly still and call to him in a low voice. After several false starts he will find you, and then such wiggling and waggling will take place as you never saw before. Pet the little fellow a bit, praise him, and put him down. Soon he will become lost again and you will have to go through the whole procedure once more—probably many times. After awhile though, as the puppy begins to learn what his nose is for, he will begin to cast about with his head down and either strike your track and trail up to you with his nose, or backtrack his own trail until he finds you. If he whines or barks on the trail while doing this, think nothing of it. Most puppies will. And most will soon cease this giving tongue on other than a game track. Some will give tongue on dog tracks, chicken tracks, horse tracks, any kind of track. Let this not worry you at this time, as most puppies will, as they mature, stop this puppy foolishness.

After the puppy has learned to overcome his fear of becoming lost, it is time enough to start his real training. Here is where you go to work. With your cane or walking stick in hand, encourage the young puppy to help you explore every likely looking tuft of grass, clump of weeds, brush pile, and overhanging creek bank—any place where a rabbit might be expected to be found. The use of the walking stick will serve a dual purpose. It will aid you in the bouncing of the bunny, and it will also accustom the young Hound to the banging of a cane on brush piles, etc. Then later, when you take him to his first field trial, he will not be frightened by the fact

149

that half the gallery will be swinging canes in an effort to get up a rabbit for the next brace.

Do not expect too much of the puppy at this stage. He is still in the kindergarten of training. If he takes off after the first rabbit you bounce, it will be surprising. Most likely he will just look after it in amazement. Mark the line as well as you can, pick up the little fellow and place his nose in the bed from whence the rabbit just fled. Then, by pointing your finger at and along the rabbit track (or line), try to encourage the pup to place his nose down and sniff at the trail. If you persevere, sooner or later, maybe a dozen rabbits later, the puppy will begin to show interest. This is the day you have been waiting for. As long as he shows interest in the line, walk along it with him so that he will not lose that interest too quickly and wander away.

Right here is a good place to remind you that some puppies start much earlier and with much less effort on the owner's part. But it is not necessarily the early or easy starter who makes the best all-age Hound. Too many times, the extremely early starter is a nervous sort of Hound, highly competitive, with a compelling desire to run, and does not in the long run make the most desirable kind of Hound. Some of the very best mature field Hounds are what we call "slow starters." Remember that no matter how well-bred puppies may be, they do not all turn out to be of championship caliber. Some do, most do not. But by careful training, most if not all Beagle pups can be transformed into good gun dogs that will give their owners many, many hours of pleasure afield and with the gun. Proper bracing, which we will touch on later, can and will help any young Hound and bring out the best qualities within him.

While the puppy is in this formative stage, it is well to teach him some manners around the barnyard and in the pastures. Walk him through the farmyard and accustom him to the sight and sound and smell of the various farm animals, the poultry, and so forth. Do not ever, under any circumstances, permit him to chase or worry the poultry or sheep. If necessary, punish him again and again. For if the pup ever gets into the habit of chasing or catching poultry

150

or sheep, it will cause you no end of trouble. You will soon find that you and your Hound are persona non grata on any farm where there is livestock or poultry. It is a natural trait for any young Hound to want to chase anything that runs or flutters before him, and the sooner you stop any interest in domestic farm animals, the better.

It is well to accustom your puppy at an early age to the close proximity of horses, for if you intend to field trial the Hound, he will, perforce, have to become accustomed to the judges' horses for the reason that most field trial judges are mounted. Many times a Hound has been forced off a trail because he was afraid of the judges' horses. Through no fault of the judge, who cannot always tell where the true line is, the judge's horse might be standing right on the line or very near it. If your young Hound has become thoroughly accustomed to horses during the training period, he will work right up under the horse's belly in an attempt to lift the line and sometimes will soundly trounce his bracemate by so doing and maybe even win himself a field trial.

By now you have probably trained the puppy to the use of a collar and leash. We like to leash-break our youngsters the easy way. That is not by trying to teach the puppy to lead while he is fresh and full of vim, vigor, and vitality, but rather, after waiting until he has most of the play out of his system. After you have had him on one of these long exploring walks and you start back toward the house or automobile, place the collar and leash on your puppy, and you will be surprised how easily he takes to it and how little resistance he puts up against the restraining leash. Very soon he will be walking along like a little gentleman, with none of the bucking and rearing that he might have put up had you tried him with the leash while he was fresh and unweary.

Most Beagles can be taught to retrieve. This is an accomplishment that will bring to your game bag many a rabbit that otherwise would have been lost. Also, it will save you many a climb up or down a steep bank or hillside or across a difficult fence. It is fairly simple to train the young Hound to pick up the dead rabbit and bring it to you. Then too, it will prevent the mangling or eating or burying of the rabbit by the Hound or Hounds, when, as so often happens, the bunny drops dead at a point beyond your vision. If the Hound has been taught to retrieve, he will have no thought of eating or mangling the corpus delicti. He will, as a matter of course, pick it up and bring it to you, unharmed.

We have found the easiest method of teaching to retrieve to be something like this: First of all, decide where the training is to be given. It must be a quiet place where there is a minimum of distracting sights and sounds. An ideal spot would be your basement. Next, you should procure a large fresh knuckle bone, too large for the youngster to get it all in his mouth. You will also need two long pieces of lightweight but strong cord, both of which should be attached to the Hound's collar.

Go to the far end of the basement with one end of a cord, and let your wife or helper remain in this end, holding the free end of the other cord. Throw the nice juicy bone a few feet away from the young Hound's nose and nature will assert itself. Any right-minded puppy will instantly go to and pick up such a tempting object as this, whereas many will show no interest whatever in *picking up* a ball or other inanimate object. As soon as the puppy takes the bone in his mouth, call to him to "fetch," at the same time exerting a gentle but steady pull on the cord. When you have drawn the youngster and his bone in to you, take the bone from him, pet him a bit, and throw the bone a few feet away from you. He will surely go for it again. Repeat and repeat, petting him and praising him each time you take the bone from him. As soon as the puppy shows signs of tiring or of losing interest in the game, stop and let him have the bone all to himself.

By repeating this procedure for a few nights, you will soon be able to throw the bone (or a fresh one, that is), farther away—even to the far end of the basement or training area. If, however, at first the puppy wants to play with you rather than to go after the bone, your helper, by using his or her cord, can gently tow the pup toward the bone. When he gets close enough to the bone, old Mother Nature will assert herself again and the young fellow will grab it in his mouth.

After not too many such lessons, you will find that you can dispense with one of the cords, and pretty soon the other cord can be removed. Be certain each time that you insist on the Beagle's relinquishing the bone to your hand. Then months later, after your pup has become well field broken and just before the gunning season opens in your area, give him a few refresher lessons. After you have made the first kill before your Hound (try like heck to kill the very first rabbit that you shoot at in front of him), follow up to the point of the kill. Encourage the youngster to pick up the dead rabbit by the coaxing use of the word "fetch." When he picks up the rabbit, back slowly away for a few feet, repeating the word "fetch." Ere long he will be bringing the dead bunny proudly to you, from increasingly greater distances, with no word of command necessary. It is questionable as to who will then be the more pleased—you, the trainer, or the puppy, the trainee.

Perhaps we have been digressing too long. Let's get back to the point in the field where the young pup, who was at that time some six or maybe even seven months old, was just beginning to show interest in the smell of a rabbit track or line. Pretty soon, and sometimes even on the first rabbit track he smells after he has begun to show interest in the scent, the youngster will "open." That is, he will bark or "give tongue" on the line. This is perhaps the highlight of the entire training period—both for you and the puppy. The chills will run up and down your back like a monkey on a stick. Don't ever think that the young Beagle doesn't like it too. Frequently, the hackles on the Hound's back will rise up like the crew-cuts on a high school football team.

Follow along behind as closely as you can because the young man, in his eagerness to get the job done all at once, will very shortly lose the line. Most generally this occurs at the first "check" or point where the cottontail made its first change in direction on the course. Being but a kindergartner, your young hopeful will be in complete darkness as to what to do next. But if you are right there with him to encourage him to stay in close to the point of loss, he will probably keep his nose to the ground and soon strike the line in the course of the new direction and carry on. If you are not up there with him, he might be prone to either start kiting all over the hillside, searching for that delectable scent, or what is more likely, to start back to the point where he remembers leaving you last.

As time goes by, he will rapidly learn how to handle himself on these checks, and as he is the only pup you are working, he will learn to do the job on his own and will not pick up any bad habits from another enthusiastic but also inexperienced young Hound, nor from an older Hound who might have faults. Soon he will be running the line for increasingly greater and greater distances. If on any of these checks he shows a disposition to run the line backwards, stop him. But before you attempt to stop him, be sure that you know what you are doing and that he is attempting to run a "backtrack." After all, he may have picked a "double," and that would make you look foolish.

This matter of backtracking is a most deplorable habit and can most generally be prevented if you are there on the job to nip it in the bud. Place yourself on the line and if the Hound starts it in reverse, scold him or switch him a bit, and encourage him to work forward in the true direction.

All Hounds do not have the same characteristic style or manner in working their checks. Even litter mates will vary widely. Some are close working and methodical in their manner. Others will want to work their checks in high gear, making wider circles in their effort to straighten out the line. The close working methodical Hound who will work in small circles at the check at a medium foot speed is the more to be desired for the reason that, generally speaking, he will "circle" his rabbit, bringing it to the gun more certainly and more quickly than will the "wide-swinging" Hound.

Encourage, if you can, patience and stick-to-it-iveness at these checks, for that is where your rabbit is run or not run, as the case may be. Most any Hound can run a rabbit to the first check. The good Hounds are the ones with the pa-

154

tience, nose, and brains to unravel the really tough checks and keep Mr. Bunny moving to the gun or to the hole.

The desire to run a rabbit is just naturally bred into the Beagle and has been for countless generations. Almost invariably that desire will come out. But as people are different, so are Beagles. Some have more desire to drive than others; some are more competitive; some have better noses; some have more "rabbit sense;" and some just plain have more common sense. In order to bring out to the best advantage all of these traits, many trips to the training field with the young Hound are indicated.

Regular work, two or three times a week if possible, with training periods of from two to three hours each, is far more to be desired than are all-day workouts at greater intervals. Like the young of all kind, your puppy will tire and lose interest if kept on the job too long at a time.

After your pride and joy has learned to circle his rabbit more often than not by himself, it is then time to give him a "bracemate." The ideal bracemate for this new beginner would be an older Hound, preferably a female—one who is not too fast on her feet, who is close working on her checks, who uses her mouth just right—not too much nor yet too little. And above all, one who has the patience to stick in close and work out those hard, really difficult, checks, where the less persevering Hound will give up and wander off in search of a new rabbit. If this older Hound, whom you are now using as a "tutor," is a driver and has the ability to always out-foot and out-check the youngster, you are in danger of ruining the young Hound. If he can constantly be out-footed, the young fellow is very likely to either become just a "me too" Hound, going along for the ride, or else his competitive spirit will become whetted to the point where he will insist on getting ahead of his older bracemate by hooking out ahead even though he does not have the line. This is a type of performance than which almost nothing could be less desired. Once a young Hound has acquired this noxious habit of hooking out ahead rather than trailing on through, it is extremely difficult, if not impossible, to break or cure him of the habit.

155

What you are after is a smooth-working team, with each Hound going only as fast as his nose will permit. In other words, with his nose geared to his feet. It is always to be remembered that this should be a smooth-working "trailing team," not a foot race.

With the young Hound now running with an older and much more experienced bracemate, the chases will be much longer and steadier, of course. But eventually they will lose, either because the rabbit "holed up" and went to ground or because it finally threw them a curve that they could not handle. It is but seldom that the Hounds run to a kill, since now, with the chase being longer, steadier, and faster, you cannot keep up. Nor is it necessary that you do so.

If possible, place yourself on an elevation of some sort near where the chase started and quietly wait, enjoying the grandest and most thrilling music on the face of God's green earth. If you are fortunate, and sometimes you will be, the rabbit will circle in such a manner as to enable you to see as well as to hear the run. When this chase finally ends as all chases must, it will most likely be the young Hound who gives up the sooner, and his first thought will be to find you and report in for re-assignment. Make it easy for him by being in the place where he remembers seeing you last —namely, at or very near the point where the last chase started. When he shows up, snap a leash on him, brag on him a bit, and wait until the old tutor shows up. It won't hurt to brag on her a bit too. She no doubt still likes a bit of petting.

Unleash the young Hound and the three of you start off in search of a new rabbit. Soon this reporting in to you at the end of a chase will become an ingrained habit with the youngster, a habit that will endure to the end of his days. A Hound that will hunt *with* you is a jewel. A self-hunter who insists on going where *he* wants to is an abominable nuisance. This is very largely a matter of early training and a matter which pays the greatest of all dividends in later years.

As you proceed slowly through the fields or woods, giving the Hounds ample time to browse about in search of a new

156

rabbit, it is well to carry on a running conversation (one-sided, of course) with your Hounds. Some people chant, some whistle from time to time in a low tone. It matters not which you do just so long as you keep the Hounds informed as to your general whereabouts and your course of direction. They will search and hunt along with you.

If you are in hilly country, try to keep both Hounds on the same side of the ridge or crest of the hill with you. If you do not, one or the other is likely to start a rabbit on the far side of the ridge, down-wind from you and the other Hound. First thing you know (or rather you won't know), the Hound is two or three ridges away from you, out of hearing, and running his heart out, while all the time you are searching for him, usually in the wrong direction. And you are wondering and worrying about where he is, if he is lost or wedged in a ground hog hole from which he cannot extricate himself.

Do not ever encourage your Hound to dig at or try to follow the rabbit into a ground hog hole or any other sort of hole after the rabbit has gone to ground. To do so is to invite trouble. At best, a Hound that spends minutes or even longer in digging at these holes will just delay the hunt. Once a Hound has developed this habit of puttering around a hole, he will continually want to return to that hole. At worst, sooner or later he will find a hole large enough that he can worm his way into it. Many Hounds have been lost forever because they got in so deep that they could not get out and their cries could not be heard.

Even if you are fortunate enough to locate him when he is stuck in one of these holes, it is no fun to have to walk miles, possibly, to where you can obtain a pick and shovel to dig him out. Besides, it makes you tired. It is far better to not let him dig at these old holes in the first place. It is true that at field trials you want your Hound to "mark hole" to the satisfaction of the judges, but it is usually not necessary for the Hound to stay at the hole but a very few minutes. The Hound does not have to go halfway to China to convince the judges that he has "marked hole."

As soon as the Hounds have convinced you that they have

Good Mover — Side View

This hound has a good free-reaching effortless stride that eats up the ground. Note (below) the space between A-B and C-D as the dog stretches out to front and rear. This is possible because the shoulders, elbows, hips, and stifles are properly placed and angulated, and so permit free movement under the chest and loins.

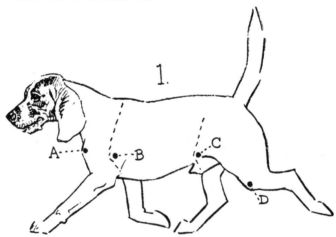

Poor Mover

This dog is not so well made and his action is short and choppy. Compare space between A-B and C-D with Beagle on the opposite page.

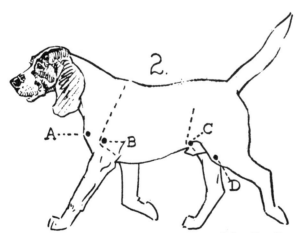

Sketch by Paul Brown, courtesy Gaines Dog Research Center

holed their rabbit, *insist* that they come away even if you have to put them on leash. Start the search for a new rabbit.

The young Hound may be hesitant when it comes to the matter of crossing running creeks or getting through woven wire fences. Never, never carry the youngster across a creek nor lift him over a fence. Cross over the creek yourself and wait on the other side. If necessary, call to the Hound. Though he may make many false starts if it is a considerable creek, usually a Hound will soon brave the water and come to you. If he is slow to come, act as if you were going to go off and leave him. Walk slowly away from the far creek bank, calling to him the while, but do not actually go off and leave him. Soon, in his frantic desire to not lose you, he will make the plunge and join you. Here again a bit of petting and praise are in order, which he will consider reward enough. After only a very few such lessons he will have absolutely no fear of the water. If you weaken and carry him across, he will long expect that service. And Brother, you will live to regret it, believe you me.

Woven wire fences are handled in much the same manner. The Hound will soon learn to clamber up a few inches to a point where the mesh is large enough to permit him to turn on his side a bit and scoot through. After a few such fence crossings, he will learn to scoot through as quick as a wink. The time that you will spend in teaching the young Hound to master these creeks and fences will save you much exasperation and many tiresome steps later, for it will not be necessary to walk back to help him across. Too, more than one Beagle field trial has been won by a Hound's superior ability to scoot through a fence with dispatch, at the exact point where the rabbit went through, while the slower and less adept bracemate was looking for a good place to get through, possibly many feet from where the rabbit went through. Obviously, if your Hound can and will go through on the line, he will not lose valuable time on the other side trying to pick up the line again.

By now your young Hound, under the tutelage of the old master, has perhaps come along to the point where he can do a pretty satisfactory job of accounting for most of his game, and the hunting season is about to open. Make certain that no guns are fired in close proximity until well after he has heard several shots fired at some considerable distance from him and while he was whole-heartedly interested in running a rabbit. If the Hounds are too close behind the rabbit when the opportunity to shoot at it occurs, let it pass. In any event, as has been mentioned before, try your level best to kill that first rabbit for him. If he is too close to you, perhaps some other member of your hunting party will have a chance to make the kill a few moments later. In no case ever let a barrage of shots be fired around this young Hound. If your hunting companions are not careful and considerate men, leave either the men or the young Hound at home.

It is our honest and firm belief that no Hound is ever born gun-shy, anymore than a child is born shy of darkness. The gun-shy Hound is made that way by careless or thoughtless humans. People who are more interested in the quick killing of a rabbit than in sensibly and gradually accustoming a young Hound to gunfire probably do not realize that a Hound's ears are much more sensitive than a human's ears. So be very careful. It is better to miss a dozen opportunities to shoot rather than ruin a good young Hound.

It won't be too long before this young fellow will not only not fear the report of a gun, he will learn truly to love it, because he will associate it with the culmination of the chase. Your problem then will be to prevent him from going to the report of a gun fired by other hunting parties in the vicinity. Good Hounds have been lost in this manner. As soon as you learn that another hunting party is near you, it is always a good idea to change the course of your hunt so as to work away from the other hunters. Your Hounds might hark to them or vice versa, and this you do not want, of course.

After killing the rabbit ahead of the young Hound, if you have not taught him to retrieve, go to the rabbit and ascertain that it is dead and therefore not suffering. Wait there until the Hounds trail their way clear up to the spot. Pick up the dead bunny and show it to them so that they will know that that particular chase has been brought to the

Good Mover, Front

Good Mover, Rear

Sketch by Paul Brown, courtesy Gaines Dog Research Center

162

Poor Mover. A Roller   Poor Mover. A Paddler

Poor Mover. Cow Hocked

Sketch by Paul Brown, courtesy Gaines Dog Research Center

ultimate conclusion. Collect your Hounds and proceed with the hunt, making certain that all of your Hounds are working forward in the same direction as you are. After all of the Hounds are well interested in the search for new game, you may stop and remove the entrails of the very recently killed bunny. Try not to let the young Hound see this operation, and under no circumstances let him eat any part of the offal; first, because most rabbits have tapeworms, and secondly, it is just plain disgusting. If your Hound starts this habit, he will spend entirely too much time in looking for offal instead of hunting, and if he eats too much he will most likely be sick on the way home in the automobile. Pleasant? By no means. After the first season of hunting, you will have very little trouble with him if you never let him get that first start

If your hunting party stops for lunch, bring the youngster in with you. It will probably be necessary to bring him in on a leash, for he will not want to stop hunting. Put him in the car or hauling container so that he too will get a half-hour's rest and be ready to go again when you are, rather than off two hills away in the wrong direction, running the tar out of a cottontail. Too, he will enjoy a light feeding of dog biscuit at lunchtime and do a better job for you in the afternoon.

Shortly after your hunting season is over, the Spring Derby Field Trials will start. It is probable that your young Beagle, who has just finished his first gunning season, will be eligible by age, as he was no doubt born during the previous calendar year. In all probability, you are so well pleased with him that you will want to enter him in a trial to see how he stacks up in competition with others. Join the Beagle club of your choice, enter your Hound, and find out. By running your Beagle at the trials, you will be able to enjoy him for almost twelve months of the year instead of just during the short gunning season.

It must be remembered that good shooting Hounds do not necessarily make good field trial Hounds. But all of the latter do make excellent shooting dogs, barring gun-shyness. When conditioning your young hopefuls for the field trials,

164

work them with only one Hound at a time. Never run them in a pack at this period. If possible, alternate the Hound's running with different bracemates of a different style or type of running, so that he will not be caught off-balance and so that he will be able to handle any sort of bracemate that he might draw at the trials.

We hope that your youngster has by now developed into a good one. You will know. If they have the proper kind of breeding behind them and the inherent ability, most will. Some, regardless of their breeding, will not be satisfactory, either to you or to the field trial judges. In this latter, not-to-be-hoped-for case, find him a good home as a pet or companion Hound and start all over again. It has been said that a man is lucky to own one good Hound in a lifetime. They do come oftener than that, and believe me, it is a thing of joy forever to own that good one.

May all of yours be GOOD!

Five Female Beagle Field Champions bred, owned, trained, and finished by Mr. and Mrs. Owen M. Payne.
Left to right, Field Champion Payne's Marsha, Field Champion Payne's Linda, Field Champion Payne's Sula, Field Champion Payne's Hilda, and Field Champion Payne's Lina.

Sandanona Beagles off on a hunt with Joint Master and Huntsman, Morgan Wing, Jr. in position.

Beagle Packs

BY MORGAN WING, JR.

COMPARATIVELY few Beaglers in America have experienced hunting with a pack of Beagles as described in this chapter. In England, however, such pack hunting has been thriving for centuries with packs maintained by individuals, schools, colleges, and the armed services.

In this country, the sport of Beagling is confined primarily to the owner of one, two, or three Beagles, who runs his Hound on cottontail rabbits for his own pleasure; shoots game (such as rabbits and pheasants) over his Beagle; or trains for the many field trials conducted by Beagle clubs under the rules of the American Kennel Club, and the club "fun" trials for members. The majority of these field trials are conducted for single Hounds to compete against one another in braces. However, there are also a number of hare trials held primarily in our Northern New England States on varying or "snowshoe" hare, in which the Hounds are entered as individuals but do run in competition together in packs. Also, a few Beagle clubs do hold two couple pack classes in which championship points are not involved, the packs usually being put together by more than one owner.

Hunting a pack in a so-called formal manner as intro-

167

SIR-SISTER BEAGLES (Red Pack)
Left, Mrs. Edward Dane, Co-Master, and right, Mrs. Henri Prunaret, First
Whip.

America's Oldest Active Beagle Pack
SIR-SISTER BEAGLES (Black Pack)
Left to right: Mrs. Henri Prunaret, First Whip; Henri Prunaret, Co-Master;
Richardson Harwood. Honorable Secretary.

duced from England many years ago means the hunting of a group of Beagles by a Huntsman with a horn, assisted by Whippers-in who are usually referred to by the less formal title of "Whip."

There are twenty active packs in the United States registered with the National Beagle Club, which is the governing body of Masters of Beagle packs as well as Bassets and Harriers. The oldest pack, the Waldingfield Beagles, established in 1886, was disbanded in 1954, and so later on was the Royal Canadian School of Infantry Beagles. The National Beagle Club, formed in 1888 as the first Beagle Club and still known as the parent club, ran its seventy-fifth annual pack trials in November 1964 at its own grounds in Aldie, Va.

The pack trials at the National are open to competition to all, though entries are primarily from the registered packs. However, to run a pack at the National, all Hounds must be the property of an individual or of a hunt organization. Classes for two, four, and eight couple are held in addition to individual stakes similar to the hare trials, except that eligibility is based on previous running in any of the other pack classes.

The registered pack is either owned and maintained financially by an individual as a private pack or supported by contributions from members and subscribers as a subscription pack. In each case there is the Master of the pack who may or may not be the same person as the Huntsman. The Master is assisted in the subscription packs by a Hunt Committee, one of the most important members of which is a Secretary-Treasurer whose duties include the sending out of the fixture cards to inform the subscribers of the place and time the Beagles will meet. It is customary for most packs to hunt at least Sunday afternoons and holidays, October through March, on the property of various landowners who have granted their permission.

The pack is a highly disciplined unit, the number making up its composition varying from five to sixteen or more couple, depending on the number of Hounds maintained by the particular hunt. The Huntsman must know his Hounds well and thus have their confidence in order to get

169

the best response from his orders. The pack is trained to such commands as "pack together," which means all Hounds gather about the huntsman in a tight group. This makes it possible to take a pack across the busiest highway in a unit, or parade a pack at the well-known Bryn Mawr Hound Show at Media, Pennsylvania, in competition for the best five couple pack. At this show one will see five or six packs presented to the judge and walked and trotted back and forth in front of one another.

In addition to certain vocal commands, there is control exercised through the use of the horn, which is the real secret to control in the field. (The horn most commonly used is the English copper or silver horn.) When the Hounds are cast, the Huntsman, through a call on his horn, keeps the unit working as a team in search for their quarry. There are various notes blown on the horn, such as a series of short rapid notes, when the cottontail or hare jumps up. All Beagles, hearing the signal, immediately rush to the Hound that has opened on the line and away the pack flies as a unit. Other notes are used when casting the pack, bringing the pack together after drawing through thick vegetation or woods, or at the time of gathering them at the end of the day. The horn can also be used to transmit information to the Whip, who may be out on a flank after a straggler. A long and short note could indicate that all the Hounds have come into the pack.

As all the packs are trained to what might be called standard commands and calls on the horn, a Master receiving an entered Beagle from another pack can expect his new Hound to have received the fundamental training which makes adjustment to running with his pack quite simple. It is interesting to see the individual three-hour pack stake at the National which is limited to two entries from each pack, for the experience will make one truly appreciate this standard training. A Huntsman is chosen to hunt the pack and though he is completely strange to all the Beagles he is hunting, with the exception of his own entry, the Hounds will cast and run for him as though they had always been together.

The Beaglers who run their Hounds in the hare stakes

The Raynham Four Couples at the National Beagle Club's 1954 trials at Institute
Farm, Aldie, Virginia.

The Raynham Beagles
(l. to r.) C. Hughes, K. H. and 1st Whipper-in; Mrs. E. H. Carle, Master and
Huntsman; Jake Carle, 2nd Whipper-in; and E. H. Carle, Secretary.

should give some thought to the use of the horn. There is always trouble in these stakes with split packs, then trying to pick up the Hounds to start again, or collecting them at the end of the stake when ordered up. The terrain in which these stakes are run is usually thick, mountainous country where the voice will not carry very far. If the horn, with a note that will carry several miles, were used, how much easier it would be to control the Beagle, not only in a pack stake but also in the field when gunning over Hounds. Though the Beagle should work fairly close to the gunner, many good Hounds have been lost when a fox or a deer carried them miles away from their starting point. Through the use of the horn there is a very good chance to recover one's hunting companion.

To appreciate pack hunting, the quarry must be discussed, for it has a distinct bearing on the conduct of the hunt. In addition to the cottontail rabbit, Beagle packs hunt the Western jack rabbit and the European hare. The jack rabbit has been introduced to the country hunted by several Eastern packs, while the European hare exists in certain parts of New Jersey, Connecticut, and New York. The European hare was imported by various sportsmen and liberated in the vicinity of their farms, the earliest importation being in 1890 in the area of Millbrook, Dutchess County, New York. This hare, which weighs from ten to fourteen pounds, gives wonderful sport for a Beagle pack, as her speed and stamina is such that she can give a run for as much as two hours or more, mostly in open farm country where one can obtain many views. The hare is fighting a real battle for existence in these States due to the fact that she is a popular target of gunners. However, the number of people interested in the preservation of this wonderful sporting animal is increasing. We can only hope that the European hare will not vanish from our countryside. The jack rabbit which thrives in many of the Western States does not propagate too well in the East and will not, because it is of a different specie, cross with the European hare. Federal law no longer permits the importation of the hare, and certain States do not sanction the release of jack rabbits, which can be readily trapped

Treweryn Beagles four couple pack at the National Beagle Club Field Trials shown with David B. Sharp, Jr., Master, and Richard Thompson, Whipper-in.

Treweryn Beagles eight couple pack at the National Beagle Club Field Trials, shown with David B. Sharp, Jr., as Huntsman, assisted by Messrs. Battin, Todd, and Thompson, as Whippers-in. .

in the West, so the pack Beaglers do have their game problems. The cottontail on which the Beagles are trained, just as are single Hounds, only give short runs, readily holing up, and do not furnish as much sport to the large group of followers of a pack.

We will assume that the pack is hare hunting on a Sunday afternoon and the Field, which corresponds to the Gallery, numbers eighty to ninety. It is not unusual for two of our large subscription packs to have over one hundred followers.

The Master is hunting the twelve couple pack which has come to the meet in the Hound truck. The Beagles have been unloaded and are quietly sitting or walking about, waiting for the short note of the horn which gives them the signal to move off. The Master and his staff, the Whips, look smart in their hunt livery of green coats with collars of the distinctive color which is their registered color, engraved brass buttons with the initials and insignia of their hunt, white stocks, white trousers, and black velvet caps. Two visitors from other packs, as determined by the color of their collars, are also attending this hunt, their hunt livery generally the same, except that one is wearing a white turtle neck sweater, white breeches, and green stockings, and the other a white shirt with tie, and khaki trousers.

The hunt livery is not worn except at the express invitation of the Master. The hunt staff is in livery in order to distinguish their positions, but certain other members of the hunt are awarded a green coat and colors from time to time in recognition of their faithful attendance and their knowledge of the sport.

As for footwear, no definite custom exists. The most practical and comfortable shoe for a long day can vary according to individual preference. The lighter, the better, and many will wear low canvas sneakers. However, a high shoe with good support is recommended for any who have any tendency to turning ankles.

The time has come to move off, and the Huntsman signals his Hounds. He walks at the head of the pack with the Whips on each flank and one in the rear to the Field which

The Royal Canadian School of Infantry Beagles, Camp Borden, Ontario, Canada, shown with Captain J. A. Gillanders, Joint Master.

Tantivy Beagles, Bennett H. Perry, Master, Henderson, North Carolina.

he will draw. The Huntsman and Whippers-in actually carry whips with an ash or leather-bound handle about twenty inches long to which is attached a leather thong three to four feet in length at the end of which is a four-inch, colored, twisted cord which makes the sharp crack when the whip is used. Whips are rarely used physically to beat a Beagle, their sole purpose being as an additional control measure. The Huntsman flicks his whip as he walks the pack in order to keep them to his rear, and the Whips do the same at the flanks if a Beagle strays to either side. If the Beagles should suddenly hit a line of a deer, the voice and the horn plus the sharp crack of the whips can often save the day by getting the Hounds' heads up long enough to stop them.

The pack has been cast and at once spreads out over the field in search of their quarry. The Huntsman has asked his Field Master (whose position and duties correspond to those of the Field Marshal) to have the Field spread out in a line behind the Hounds so that they can help put up the hare which squats in the open in her form and can often be passed over by the pack. Most of the hare or jacks are initially jumped up by a member of the Field as the Hounds can cover only a small portion of the large territory hunted.

In order to complete the best coverage possible, the Huntsman should zig-zag, that is, cast the Hounds back and forth, parallel to those who are following the pack, and at least fifty yards in front. On their part, the Field must not get too close to the Beagles so as to press them or hurry them while searching. The Huntsman who casts his Hounds as described will not only have a better opportunity to put up a hare, but also will give the Field more enjoyment than by walking straight through a pasture or plowed field. His followers will be closer to the working pack and will have a better chance to participate in the thrill of the first view of the hare.

The Beagles are working a hillside near a small thicket when a cottontail suddenly bounds forth into a nearby wood. As we desire to hunt only hare this afternoon, a Whip quickly cracks his whip while the Master sounds a few sharp

OLD CHATHAM HUNT FOOT BEAGLES

Garbed in their traditional hunting costumes, the hunt staff looks over their Hounds prior to a meet at Balintra Farms. *Left to right,* Hugh McB. Johnston, Henry Gammack, S. Napier Smith, Whippers-in; A. S. Callan, Jr., Honorary Huntsman; and Mrs. Henry Gammack, Master.

The Buckram Beagles, shown with Huntsman and Joint Master Joseph B. Connolly, Jr., center; Barbara H. Conolly, Whip, *left*; and Clinton G. Bush Jr., Whip, *right*. In the *left back* is J. Wooderson Glenn, Joint Master, leading the field; at *far right* are Ann D. Conolly, Whip, and Owen D. Frisbie, Secretary.

notes on his horn, and soon the pack is back together and proceeding with their business.

The owner of the property has heard the commotion and looks from his living room window to see what is going on. He immediately recognizes the green coats among the large group of people and knows that the Beagles are afoot and that it is not an invasion of hunters on his property. He knows that the followers of the Beagle pack have received instructions to respect his property from the point of view of avoiding damage (instructions such as climbing the fences at the post to avoid breaking a rail and keeping to edges of sown fields if the ground is not frozen). He comes forth to observe the fun.

The Master decides to try the plow to his left and signals with his arm the direction in which he will cast the Hounds so that his Whips and followers will be alerted to his forty-five degree change in the axis of his draw. The use of arm signals can be most helpful, for in this case the Whip on the left will pivot with the pack, while the Whip on the right has some extra running to do.

As the pack enters the plow, suddenly new life seems to bubble forth from the little Beagles, their gaily waving sterns (called feathering), being the barometer of their enthusiasm. A few start to whimper as their excitement grows. Tally-ho! A hare jumps forth from a furrow and streaks off with the pack in full cry and the Master giving the rapid notes of "Gone Away" on the horn. The Field springs to life and the youngsters stretch forth their legs behind the flying pack while the older members, playing the game in a cagey manner, head for the high ground to observe which way the pack is swinging.

At the first welcome check, after a blistering run of over a mile, all Hounds are suddenly silent as their heads go down and they methodically work a hedgerow. Gradually, a few members of the Field arrive, and if they are regular followers, they know they should stand still and keep quiet for this is a crucial moment. Loud talking and other such disturbances can mean the lifting of the Hounds' heads at a time when all must be working to unravel the scent which under certain conditions remains for only a very little time. On cold windy days, for example, the scent will be dissipated within an extremely short period of time.

Farther down the hedgerow, a member of the Field is seen approaching. He suddenly stops, watches for a moment, then raises his hat in the direction of the adjacent field, indicating that he has viewed the hare. The Master slowly works his pack toward this person and asks him some questions, as the pack does not yet acknowledge the line. To be most helpful at this point, one should be able to give this basic information: the direction or last point at which the hare was seen, how long ago, and the direction in which she was heading. The Master quickly takes advantage of the information and lifts the pack, by using his voice and horn, to a point on the other side of the hedgerow where with a crash of music the pack opens. Not all the Field have yet caught their breath, but the check has helped and away they go, spurred on by the intriguing "come on" music of the Hounds.

The pack swings toward a fairly busy road, and the Whip cuts as fast as he can toward this highway to stop cars should the hare cross. When a pack is on the line, the Hounds in their excitement have no other thought than to pursue their quarry. Across the highway, the pack takes us to the bank of a good-sized stream, where another check occurs. The Beagles work along the bank while one finally plunges in and swims to the other side. This Beagle opens and the pack braves the cold water to rush eagerly to their teammate. The Master had not expected this hare to take to water, but she has, so in we go, knee deep, drawn on by the music of the Hounds. The sun begins to sink and the Hounds have driven their hare for one hour and twenty minutes over approximately six miles of countryside.

It has been a fast pace, and everyone is wet and cold after the stream crossing, so it is decided to call it a day at the next check. The Master blows long notes on his horn indicating the end of the day, and with some help from the Whips, who have called "pack together," all twelve couple are about the Master within a few minutes to start the long weary walk back to the place of the meet.

To the Beagler who wonders how such unity is achieved in this type of pack Beagling, let us direct a discussion of the training of the pack Hound. First, the young Hound is broken to a lead, then to coupling. The youngster is then coupled to an older, thoroughly trained member of the pack, and along with six or seven youngsters also thus coupled, is given road work. This training usually takes place during the spring and summer months, the young Hounds averaging about one year of age, and being prepared to enter the pack that fall. A dozen walks, covering several miles, will often be sufficient to teach basic pack manners. While walking the Beagles, the trainer will do well to have his pockets loaded with biscuits to serve as rewards when the Hounds perform with exceptional merit. In addition, the trainer should encourage the young Hounds with words and pats, always giving the command of "pack together" with firmness. The older Hound will draw the young Beagle to the trainer, and it will not be long before this command is known.

Other commands can be similarly taught, such as "road over" to get the pack to group to the side of the road should a car be coming along. Some young Hounds will learn faster than others, so as they are released to walk with the pack, they should be watched closely, for it will surely be necessary to couple up two or three again for further walks with their mentors.

A very important part of the training of the young pack Beagle is to walk the pack past farm yards to expose the inexperienced Hound to as many animals as possible—chickens, sheep, cattle, cats, and other dogs. If in their early training the Hounds are taught to ignore such animals, it will prevent the pack from "rioting" on farm animals when their attention should be centered on the line they are following. A pack may also "riot" while hunting rabbits or hare if pheasants, for example, are flushed and the attention of the Hounds is distracted from their rightful quarry. Should this happen, one may hear "Ware Wing," the terminology used in such cases by many Masters.

A pack may walk well together, but, more important, it must run together as a close unit. After the pack has settled to the line, ideally, one should be able to apply the well-known expression, they can be "covered by a blanket." This uniformity in running speed can only be achieved by continuous "heading and tailing," that is, eliminating the fast and the slow Hounds. Many a good Hound must be sold to accomplish this end. The size of the Beagle does not necessarily determine the speed, for there is many a thirteen-inch Beagle that can outfoot a slow fifteen-inch Beagle; consequently, it is normal to have a pack mixed in size. However, as another point of perfection, it is desirable to match the pack as nearly as possible in size, type, appearance, and color, and as to melodiousness of voice. Consequently, to develop a "dream pack," a Master has a lifetime job ahead of him.

He must draft out of his pack the leader who is too strong and dominating for the others, the babbler, the cheater or jealous Hound, the skirter, the Hound who does not speak enough, and the backtracker. After this, he can think about color, selling his lemon and white or very open-marked Hounds if solid blankets are his preference. However, a few light-colored Beagles will help spot the pack when one is far behind and has painfully gained a hilltop.

The Master must have in his pack a Hound or two with good strong voices which makes the pack rush to them at the check. One or two good road Hounds, particularly for hare hunting, can be most helpful, as both jack rabbit and hare will use paths and roads wherever possible.

All of this cannot be accomplished at one time. It takes years to build a pack, but there is such a challenging goal in the approach of the perfection the pack Master seeks. It is not by chance that the Master develops the pack that will win on the bench and in the field. It is possible to have a few lucky breedings, but what happens from that point? A knowledge of genetics, plus an intuition or "feel," along with some experimentation are required. Will line breeding, inbreeding, or an outcross bring the pack the desired voice or closeness on the line? The desired result will not always be obtained even through the intelligent application of hard-gained knowledge, practical experience, and theoretical principles, for the ideal Hound cannot be produced with a mechanical exactitude.

This chapter has been written to try to give all who are not familiar with Beagle packs some knowledge of this little-known segment of the Beagle world. To show that there are several paths open to the Beagler, I. W. ("Ike") Carrel, editor of the monthly Beagle magazine, *Hounds and Hunting,* at every opportunity presents news of packs in his columns.

To the Beagler who runs his Hounds in single braces where the Hound must not be handled once he is running the cottontail against his bracemate, it is often very difficult to understand the pack classes in which the voice, the horn, and the Whips can help at a check. The pack Beagles are bred and trained to handle. The pack Masters want and need discipline when hunting a large pack. The same principle applies to the two couple pack in competition. To bring about the best team work, for which the pack Masters strive, the two couple pack must be hunted in the same manner as the four and eight couple packs. On the other hand, one often hears other Beaglers say, "Wish my Beagle would handle that way."

The pack membership of the National Beagle Club is ready to help anyone who is interested in starting a pack of Beagles by providing Hounds at a special price. A new pack which starts with Beagles from a few well established packs will get off to a much faster start than if Hounds are obtained from non-pack sources. Registration rules and other details may be obtained from the Secretary, Morgan Wing, Jr., Millbrook, New York.

Packs of Beagles have been maintained in this country for short periods at several schools and universities. They did not survive, for in each case their existence depended on the enthusiasm and leadership of one or two individuals who graduated or left the faculty. What a grand, healthy sport would be provided for any school, university, or college, whether girls' or boys', were Beagle packs maintained for the students to enjoy.

As stated at the outset, in England such packs are maintained. Famous packs of two well-known and leading universities are Christchurch and New College (Oxford), which celebrated in 1952 their one hundredth hunting season, and Trinity Foot (Cambridge), formed in 1862. There are many service packs—Army, Navy, and Air Force—maintained not only by units such as regiments and brigades but also there are packs at service academies of learning such as the Aldershot Beagles, which pack started hunting in 1870, and the Sandhurst Beagles (maintained by the Royal Military Academy, which corresponds to our United States Military Academy at West Point). The service packs provide good relaxation, sport, and physical training. The idea of service packs has at last crossed the Atlantic Ocean in our direction, for this past year the National Beagle Club was pleased to welcome a new pack, the Royal Canadian School of Infantry Beagles, whose kennel is located in Camp Borden, Ontario, approximately sixty miles north of Toronto, near Barrie. Camp Borden is a training center for several thousand men and participation in the Beagle pack has been made a part of the physical education program.

English school packs are maintained in various ways. For example, at the Downside School, which started its pack in 1945, the headmaster appoints one of the boys as Master. The Master then arranges his own hunt and kennel staff. There is no kennelman employed, the boys doing all of the work. Membership in the pack is open to outsiders, but the main purpose is to provide a healthy occupation and recreation for those boys who are interested in animals and in country life.

The twenty Beagle packs registered with the National Beagle Club, together with the names and addresses of the Masters, are as follows:

Name of Pack	Estab-lished	Master and Kennel	Color of Collar
Adrossan Beagles	1961	Rober M. Scott St. David's, Pa.	Blue, Brown Piping
Black Mountain Beagles	1959	Stuart Auchincloss and Mrs. F. Myra Engman Santa Cruz, Calif.	Scarlet, White Piping
Buckram Beagles	1934	John W. Oelsner Brookville, L.I., N.Y.	Grey
Cedarcroft Beagles	1958	James G. Lamb, Jr. Chester Springs, Pa.	Antique Gold
Fairfield County Beagles	1961	T. F. Gilroy Daly and Mrs. Quentin De Streel Westport, Conn.	Apple Green
Fox Hill Beagles	1965	S. D. Drewry DeFord Richmond, Va.	Lemon
Ligonier Valley Beagles	1954	William R. Oliver and William C. O'Neil Ligonier, Pa.	Blue
Liseter Beagles	1928	Mrs. J. Austin duPont and John E. duPont Newtown Square, Pa.	Dark Blue, Light Blue Piping
Little Prospect Beagles	1952	Mr. and Mrs. Anthony N. B. Garvan and Roger Hillas, Spring House, Pa.	Robins Egg Blue, Black Piping
Merry Beagles	1959	Mrs. Myron E. Merry Gates Mills, Ohio	Yale Blue, Green Piping
M.O.C. Beagles	1961	Mrs. Paul Fout The Plains, Va.	White
Nantucket-Treweryn Beagles	1924	Mr. and Mrs. David B. Sharp, Jr., Exton, Pa.	Maroon, White Piping

Name of Pack	Estab-lished	Master and Kennel	Color of Collar
North Country Beagles	1953	The late Charles K. Backus (new Master not appointed) Metamora, Mich.	Gold, Black Piping
Old Chatham Hunt Foot Beagles	1953	Albert S. Callan, Jr. and John S. Williams, Jr. Kinderhook, N.Y.	Yellow, Dark Green Piping
Rocky Fork Beagles	1954	E. Craig Delong and Daniel Howland Gahanna, Ohio	Gentian, Light Blue Piping
Sandanona Beagles	1948	Oakleigh B. Thorne and Morgan Wing, Jr. Millbrook, N.Y.	Yellow, Grey Piping
Sir Sister Beagles	1909	Mr. and Mrs. Henri Prunaret, Natick, Mass.	Hunting Scarlet
Tanheath Beagles	1959	William A. Albin Uxbridge, Mass.	Buff, Gold Piping
Wolver Beagles	1913	C. Oliver Iselin, Jr. Middleburg, Va.	· Buff, Light Blue Piping
Woodfield Beagles	1950	Mrs. Gilbert Humphrey and G. Watts Humphrey Chagrin Falls, Ohio	Light Blue, Black Piping

Litter of Beagle puppies by CH. MERRY CHASE JESTER ex
CH. MERRY CHASE DOLL.

185

CH. SOGO SHODOWN

CH. SOGO MASTERPIECE

186

Glossary of Beagling Terms

Account for: To kill the rabbit, or to run it to earth.

All-Age Class: Class for Hounds of any age.

Anchor Hound: Hound that holds back at checks.

Babbler: Hound that barks continuously when trailing; also, Hound that is given to false tonguing.

Backtrack: Run in the direction from which the game has come.

Blank: Area in which no rabbit (or other game) is found.

Blue tick: A Hound whose coat has a bluish cast resulting from small patches of dark hair on light background—may be said of the entire coat, or coloration may appear only on part of the body.

Brace: Two Hounds running or hunting together.

Bracemate: Hound competing in a brace.

Bye Hound: The odd Hound in any class who lacks a bracemate because there are an uneven number of Hounds competing.

Carry a line: To follow scent well.

Cast: The swing or circle made in attempting to recover the line of scent at a check.

Check: Temporary loss of scent.

Clean Hound: One without faults.

Close Hound: One which stays close to the line of scent, particularly under difficult trailing conditions.

Coarse: Voice of poor quality.

Cold line: Line of scent difficult to follow because it is old, or because trailing conditions are poor.

Cold trailing: Open on scent made long enough before that trailing is difficult.

Couple: A leash or fastener for holding two Hounds together; also, two Hounds in a pack. In this sense, couple is the term commonly used to describe the total number of Hounds in a pack (e.g., a two couple pack would consist of four Hounds, a four couple pack of eight Hounds, etc.).

Crash: The pack giving tongue together.

Cry: The voice or tongue when a Hound is running on the line.

Cull: Process of eliminating the less desirable Hounds; also, those eliminated.

Cut and slash: Weave across line of scent; also, overrun, causing unnecessary checks.

Derby: A Beagle is a derby during the year in which he was whelped and the calendar year following the year in which he was whelped.

Derby trial: Trial in which entries are limited to Beagles in the derby class.

Die, or die on trail: Lose the scent.

Double: When a rabbit stops and reverses direction, running back over its original trail.

Drag: Artificial trail.

Drag Hounds: Hounds used on artificial trail.

Draw: Search for game in specific area.

Drawing: Selection of Hounds to be run together as bracemates.

Earth: Burrow which rabbit appropriates to escape Hounds.

Entry: A competitor in any class; also first season Hound joining a pack (e.g., young entry).

Fault: Poor technique, or poor conformation.

Field: Spectators at trial.

Flag: White part of Beagle's tail.

Flier: Hound of exceptional trailing ability.

Form: The rabbit's squat or bed.

Fresh trail: One made recently.

Futurity: Term applied to certain specially nominated Hounds competing during year following their derby age.

Gallery: Spectators.

Game: Quarry in any chase.

Gap: Break in line of scent.

Ghost runner: Hound following imaginary scent.

Giving tongue: Term used to describe the Hound's use of his voice when running on trail.

Gone to ground: Term used to describe rabbit's entering of underground shelter.

Hare Stakes: Type of competition in which all Hounds in a class compete together in a pack after hare.

Hark: Command for other Hounds to join Hound barking on line of scent.

Hark forward: Term employed by Huntsman to encourage Hounds to go forward.

Hark in: Term used to describe action of Hound that joins bracemate who has started game and gives tongue.

Heads up: Term used to describe Hounds' raising heads from ground in seeking scent.

Heat: The contest between a brace of Hounds.

Heavy voice: Voice that is loud and carries well.

Heeler: Hound that follows at heel and is therefore poor searcher.

Hit off: Recover the line of scent at a check.

Hold hard: Term used as warning to spectators to stay back and not press closely toward Hounds.

Honor a line: Verify bracemate's note by tonguing the line of scent.

I. B. F.: International Beagle Federation.

Jump Hound: One which is a good starter.

Jumping: Term used to describe the starting of rabbits.

Kill: Term used to describe the act of catching the quarry.

Lay on: Start Hounds on scent.

Lift: Take Hounds from point where scent is weak or lost, and place them at point farther along the line of scent.

Light Hound: One whose voice is not as loud as the average Hound; also, Hound physically lacking in bone structure.

189

Line: The actual trail of the quarry, as indicated by his scent.

Line stealer: Hound which runs from check until he is well ahead of bracemate before giving tongue.

Looper: Hound that makes looping casts when running.

Loss: Any given point at which Hounds can no longer find scent of rabbit. A permanent check.

Marked line: Trail on which game has been sighted.

Marking hole: Term used to describe Hound's digging and/or barking at point where rabbit has gone to ground.

Marshals: Officials at trials whose duties consist of carrying out instructions from judges and field trial committees.

Meet: The place at which people gather for a hunt.

Mouthy: Unnecessarily noisy.

Mute: Hound which is silent on trail.

Noisy Hound: One given to excessive use of voice, or one which gives voice when not making progress on the line.

Nose: Ability to scent.

Open: Term used to describe Hound's first indicating by use of his voice that he has scented rabbit on new line.

Open marked: Spotted or irregular coat coloration with white predominating.

Ordered up: Term used to describe judges at trials asking handlers to catch their Hounds because they have finished judging.

Overrun: Run beyond check, or beyond point at which scent is discernible.

Pack: A group of more than two Hounds running together.

Pack sense: Term used to describe ability of Hounds to run well together.

Pack Stake: Class at trial in which more than two Hounds are run together.

Picker: Hound which follows trail slowly and methodically.

Pottering Hound: One which dwells on scent without making progress.

Quarry: Any hunted animal.

Quiet Hound: One which does not give tongue sufficiently when following line of scent; well behaved.

Re-cast: Start afresh in Pack Stake.

Riot: Term used to describe Hounds' running something other than designated quarry.

Routing: Jumping game.

Running heel: Backtracking.

Run out: Term used to describe Hound's failure to stay with bracemate.

Run out of rabbit: To lose line of scent.

Skirter: Hound that cuts corners or that runs wide of pack.

Slash: Cut corners at difficult points on line.

Slasher: Hound that fails to stay on line because he runs too rapidly.

Split: Term used to describe Hounds' separating from each other to follow two different rabbits.

Squat: Rabbit's nest; also, place where rabbit stops suddenly and crouches, attempting to hide from Hounds.

Start: Find game or trail of game.

Strike: Find game or trail of game.

Strike Hounds: Those which find game readily.

Swing: Cast about in attempt to recover the line of scent at a check.

Tail Hounds: Hounds at rear of pack.

Tally-ho: Signal indicating that game has been sighted and that Hounds are to begin chase.

Tight-mouthed: Lacking sufficient voice.

Tongue: The Hound's voice.

Viewed away: Term used to describe the fact that the game has been seen going away.

Voice: The Hound's bark.

Weaving: Working back and forth, from side to side, on a line.

Whipper-in: The individual who acts as the Huntsman's assistant in an organized pack.

Wide: Overrun at turns and checks.

Working a line: Following a scent.